To Greg, and never leaving projects u
Selah.

Contents

Forward

Not all Christmases are created equal.

One of the most magical Christmas experiences I've ever had, happened in Bergen Norway in the early 2000's. My husband and I were guests (and our young family), of friends who were going back home to the snowy northern regions of Europe, for two luxurious weeks. Norwegians certainly know how to do Christmas. I mean why wouldn't they? The bearded man himself is from around those parts! Most people use "jul" to refer to the week stretching from Christmas Eve to New Year's Eve. Every item in the supermarket is labelled with a "jul" before the food type (i.e., jul bread); the build-up is not just a typical western haze of crazy last-minute shopping, there are traditions and specific things to cook and eat on the days leading up to Christmas. The trees are huge, the lights shine bright, and there is a constant smell of wood burning stoves and authentic spruces in the air. I think probably one of my favourite things about a Norwegian Christmas is that they have a term for "that time between Christmas and New Year when no-one is really sure what they should be doing." This time is referred to as *romjul*, and I shall use it forever more!

Christmas Eve is the "big day" and as my young family and I walked out of the early evening church service with sleepy, snuggled up children, the snow began to fall. Snow. On Christmas Eve. I tilted my face up to the sky, and I wanted to cry. I was overwhelmed with the beauty and magic of it all broken up into the angelic, white dust falling upon my nose and forehead. Isn't this what we all want; to feel that tinge or totality of Christmas spirit separating us from the hustle and bustle of the commercialised festivities we've always known and endured?

Christmas has meant many things to me over the years. Christmas has highlighted my lack; my lack of money, thought and organisation. My lack of care for things loud and busy. My lack of desire for sparkly dresses, and drinks. I'm mostly known for being dragged into Christmas quietly moaning

"No, not again!"

At the same time, I am deeply touched by the story, I am captivated by the light. I have a visceral response to children singing "Away in a manger" in an old school hall whilst I'm sat on an uncomfortable plastic chair.

I first met Serena in the late 1990's; we were young dreamers and doers. We shared an affinity for baguette's, brie cheese and a handful of grapes at lunch. Serena exuded life from the first time we met. I have subtly attempted to siphon her powers of wisdom, intellect, and creativity ever since. I make it my duty in life to surround myself with readers and beauty seekers. Serena McCarthy leads the way, with a blazing trail! Serena is a gatherer. Serena is a nurturer and hostess who welcomes you in with open arms. She does not have time to stand on ceremony, so please, come just as you are. I've been the recipient of Serena's hot coffee, sweet potato tacos and fine wine many times. Reading *Signs of Christmas* exuded the same warmth of her hospitality; her writing welcomes us in and reminds us that there's no need to pretend anymore. We are all at this Christmas party together, ready, or not.

When you are a friend of Serena, you become a rightful recipient of her stories. Her experiences and anecdotes are woven into the legacy of her life. Her words have woven festive meaning into mine. Her tales have taught me to be intentional, to soak up the stillness, to get up and out and make something happen; to do simple things repeatedly, painting the narrative from Nazareth like a banner, over many Christmases to come.

Reading *Signs of Christmas* has given me a fresh perspective on the festive season, with a hope to build again, after not always embracing it enthusiastically. Serena not only inspires with stories from her own life, but she also shares history, meaning and insight into the traditions and practices that we so often take for granted. Serena's writing is reflective of her reading life, but I also deeply appreciate her film analogies; especially as she refers to a favourite of mine, "Love Actually" where a young primary school age girl plays a lobster in the age-old nativity play. What a hoot!

On the pages of this beautiful book Serena shares truth and points us to beauty. She doesn't indulge us with glittery idealism and far-reaching fairy tales, but she does lead us to a place of contemplation and reflection. She invites us to consider how we can gently adjust how we see and celebrate the Christmas season, in the light of our own unique lives.

Signs of Christmas guides the reader through song, story, research, and real-life situations that I'm sure we can all relate to and remember (being the narrator in the school play, yep - that was me too). Keep this book in a place where you sit with your coffee and Christmas candle every morning; open the pages and treat yourself to an essay a day (if you can't resist reading on) as you prepare and hang with pride, your own signs of Christmas.

God bless us, everyone!

Leah Boden

Introduction

The Lamp is burnin' low upon my tabletop
The snow is softly fallin'
The air is still in the silence of my room
I hear your voice softly callin'

In November of 2020, I was on a video call with my dear friends Dan and Kerstin. The conversation, as it so often does with these friends, turned to the church and our plans for Advent services. Dan mentioned his sermon series was entitled The Signs of Christmas. It started a little journey in my brain. What, for me, are the signs of Christmas? What thoughts and stories do they conjure in my mind? We were plunged into a second lockdown the next day and I found my thoughts exploring further as the idea of a different type of Christmas began to come into my mind. Later that same day, a friend sent me a photograph of my first book of carols from my days as an elementary piano student. They had found it in their house, and I had not seen it for at least twenty-five years. The picture on the front cover and the space inside the front cover, where I had inscribed 'Serena-Mary McCarthy age 8,' transported me back to that time in my life. The ideas all fell into place. I decided to write an Advent blog, on four of the signs of Christmas. I have had these ideas before, why I followed through on this one, remains a mystery. I ran out of weeks before I ran out of ideas. In order to keep busy through the rest of the winter whilst we were in the midst of another lockdown, I decided to use my spare time to put this little book together. And here we are with this little book. That is a very long diatribe of how this book came to exist.

When I think about why it exists, it is because I find Christmas to be exhausting. There is so much going on, during the winter months. As I wrote the Advent blog, and into January and February, I held up the pieces of our Christmas traditions, the weird and the wonderful, and looked at them in their own light and in their own time. I found, as is often the case, that the parts have meaning. I found them rich with meaning and inspirational in helping me to craft a more meaningful Christmas season.

This book of Christmas thoughts aims to help us reframe what we do at Christmas, to take us on a journey exploring the roots of some of our traditions and making some suggestions toward having a more meaningful Christmas. A more hospitable Christmas. A more communal Christmas, one that considers the least, the last and the wanderers.

 A place for everything and everything in its place. That's the key to a tidy home, a tidy mind, and a fulfilled life. The problem is things, people and ideas do not like to stay in their place. Christmas is the vilest offender. A few years ago, I was looking for some chocolate coins; to use as an illustration for a school assembly. As I walked into the Supermarket, I was convinced they would not be available, yet there they were in the Christmas aisle, in September. The following week, I saw the child of a friend sitting on the couch, looking wistfully into the air. I asked what they were doing. They responded in an ethereal way 'just sitting here, waiting for Christmas.' Christmas does not like to stay in its place, and because of that, its potency is diluted.

Now don't get me wrong, I am all about Christmas. I love it, but I love it in its proper place. I used to love the artificial barrier that Thanksgiving provided when I lived in the States. After Thanksgiving, the community I lived in went Christmas crazy. However, in the last few years, the signs of Christmas would start to be visible before the last bite of the pumpkin pie had been digested. It would start to spread itself from almost the beginning of September. You would see hints of decorations, and preparations and I just wanted to yell No! Keep Christmas special, keep it in its place.

Advent, the period between Thanksgiving and Christmas, is the season of waiting. It is the season of patient expectation. A season to look and wait for the signs of Christmas. The signs of songs, of light, of trees and angels and much more. Join me, as we explore them together. Selah.

Lights

Those Christmas lights
Light up the street
Down where the sea and city meet
May all your troubles soon be gone
Oh, Christmas lights keep shining on
Those Christmas lights
Light up the street
Maybe they'll bring her back to me
And then all my troubles will be gone
Oh, Christmas lights keep shining on
Oh, oh, oh, oh, oh, oh, oh
Oh, Christmas lights
Light up the street
Light up the fireworks in me
May all your troubles soon be gone
Those Christmas lights keep shining on

Those December days when the darkness lengthens. When the world never quite seems to wake up. Cloud upon cloud upon dull, grey, cloud. Endless grey and then, you spot them. One house then another. A tree, a lighted reindeer. Until the streets dance with light, on the dullest December day.

I do love them, but they have always seemed a little odd. We put lights outside our house and then go inside, close the curtains, and have another mince pie. Oblivious to the spectacle we have created outside. Christmas lights, in the gardens and windows of houses are the most other centred behaviour in this self-centred culture and season. Lights are the one thing that we do each year that is almost entirely for our neighbour. It is a generous act, that says, this darkness will not have the last word. It is an act of rebellion against selfishness. It requires the sacrifice of time and electricity for the benefit of others. Beyond a glimpse, as we rush inside, laden down with shopping bags, we scarcely see the lights on the outside of our homes.

The more I think about it the more I realise that as much as they are for a community, they are a community in and of themselves. If you will forgive the obvious and slightly prosaic personification, I will explain. They rely on each other; lights only work if each individual light remains connected to the source. Have you ever experienced the frustration of trying to achieve the impossible and getting a string of lights to work? Making sure that each twinkling light is screwed in tightly. Often, it seems easier to throw the whole string away and purchase a new set. You know the fancy ones with a set of switches that flicker and dim in exciting patterns. Or LED ones that are lighted in different colours. It is definitely easier to make this purchase rather than repairing the community of lights that we already possess and helping a mischievous or disconnected light return to its source. It is much simpler to throw them away and splurge on the cash to purchase a new set. The trouble is, at the first sign of trouble with the new string we will be quick to discard them having created a habit or pattern of throwing away something, rather than endure the frustrating task of reconnecting something to the source.

Sometimes, after a long time, the cable becomes frayed and bare wires show the green outer casing. We must, at that moment, decide if the electrical tape we are placing over frayed wires can repair them to working order. This action takes time, but it is worth it if it means that connection can be restored, and light can be maintained.

Some friends have a set of Christmas lights that are at least fifty-five years old. They purchased them the year they had their Victorian house wired with thirteen-amp plugs. They are held together with electrical tape and love. There is always some applause when they are finally plugged in each winter and flicker to life. During the past 20 years I have shared Christmas meals with a group of friends. No gifts, no faff, just a Christmas meal and some, actually, a lot of drinks each December. We are frayed and worn. We have laughed and cried together. We are held together by electrical tape, love, and a kick-ass Clementini, thanks, Rachel. Each year we are a little greyer, and each year this tradition is more of a highlight of the Christmas season than the previous year. If we had given up on our friendship at the first sign of trouble or when one of us did not shine so brightly, the highlight would have been short-lived. Perhaps, we need to start to think about our communities like a string of Christmas lights. It only works if they remain connected to each other and to the source.

Could it be that this, our first sign of Christmas, is the closest to the real meaning of Christmas that we will explore on our journey? A light in the darkness. A light in the darkness, entirely for the sake of others. A light in the darkness, to prove that darkness will end; all the darkness that there ever was will be swallowed by light. Put your lights up with fresh abandonment this year. Brighten the day for someone else and look for space to be like a light everywhere you go this season. Selah

Advent

O come, O come, Emmanuel,
And ransom captive Israel,
That mourns in lonely exile here
Until the Son of God appears.
Rejoice! Rejoice! Emmanuel
shall come to thee, O Israel.

It is late Summer 2021; I have just returned home from a trip to the Isle of Wight. Whilst there I saw someone building a Taj Mahal sandcastle. With international travel still restricted, I suppose this endeavour is one way to visit exotic destinations. The very next afternoon I saw Christmas cake available in the free-from aisle. This disturbs me on many levels. Christmas cake is, in my opinion, an oddly endured delicacy, and if I were a coeliac, I would play my gluten-free card willingly if I was offered some cake. I am not sure whether the Taj Mahal sandcastle or the gluten-free Christmas cake is more ridiculous. Friends and family who work in retail are beginning to feel the pressure of the Christmas season and I have not put my shorts away yet. In fact, it is a balmy 27 degrees (80 degrees Fahrenheit) today.

We seem to rush to the celebration of Christmas. I understand it from a financial perspective, for both businesses and the consumer, it does spread the cost a little bit. Although, I have definitely had to purchase some Christmas chocolate twice, because, well, I will leave that to your imagination.

I think this rush to the celebration, to get to the good bit as quickly as possible, is indicative of our desire to make the outcome a certainty. We want to rid the world, in every situation we can control, of tension. We are not very good at managing or handling tension. We solve issues on the easiest side of easy. Can't be bothered to cook? Buy a takeaway, problem solved. Need a pick me up? Online shopping means we are no longer restricted by opening hours. I recently saw an advert for a workout vest that meant you only had to do a twenty-minute workout each week to achieve the body of your dreams. Surely, anything that can be achieved in twenty minutes can be lost again as quickly. What about the challenges we cannot solve the easy way I hear you ask? Well, we either numb them completely, which is what we collectively did with Covid, by spending an unprecedented amount of money on takeaways, online shopping, chocolate, and alcohol. The other option, which is what we do at Christmas, is to skip right to the celebration. But I think we miss something in this choice, we miss the depth of our need as humans and as a result, we miss the depth of our delight in discovering the solution.

Advent means 'coming' as in waiting for something to arrive. It comes from the Latin root 'Adventus' which is where we receive the word adventure from as well. Waiting is an adventure. What happens in our being while we are forced to wait, or when we are in a situation where the outcome is uncertain, is intrinsic to our development as compassionate human beings. It is, as it were, an adventure for the soul. Choosing kindness, in a moment of tension is an adventure. Choosing to hope or have peace amid an unsure outcome is also an adventure. Joy is an adventure. When so many of our circumstances dictate the opposite. Our frustrations, disappointments, and anger at the fluctuation in Christmas planning 2020 revealed just how much we need an Advent. *

A season of tension, waiting and unsure outcomes A season of silent expectation. The adventure of joy, peace, and hope when our collective circumstances have been radically altered. It would be good. I am convinced, it would be good for our souls

These virtues are those that we celebrate or remember each year, in the weeks of Advent. Peace, Joy, Hope and Faith. All of which are anchors to our soul, mind, and body when the outcome is uncertain. Without them, if we skip ahead to Christmas day without the waiting period, we lose these anchors and float on a sea of desires, which will easily carry us away.

There was certainly a year when I skipped the waiting process, and from my memory, it became the worst Christmas ever. I was about ten years of age. I found the present stash in my parents' wardrobe. After a few days of dreaming about them, I crept into the wardrobe and nicked tiny holes in all the presents. I knew everything. I felt like God, with all the knowledge and power. That is, until Christmas morning, when there were no surprises, nothing that captured my imagination. I determined then and there not to be the present ripper and to enjoy the sense of expectation. I embraced Advent for everything that it contained. Natural consequences did their part, at that moment. However, I still have the reputation of being the present ripper in my family stories. I thought the statute of limitations was less than thirty years. However, it seems that in this situation, as in so many others, I was wrong.

However witty and complex my childhood may have been, this little book is about signs of Christmas and the question remains, how can we reclaim this season of Advent? This season our soul needs; when so much messaging pushes us to skip the tension of Advent and shortcut to the celebration. Like so many things, I do not know the answer. I do know that as recently as the 1950's the Advent season was similar in nature to the Lenten fast, a way to make sure we are good and hungry for the feasting season of the twelve days of Christmas. The season which a dear friend refers to as, the season of brown food. For the record, it is also the only season of the year when I allow pork pie and Twiglets to pass my lips.

Advent calendars certainly help, and before you label me as 100% Grinch, even the chocolate ones. I might even go as far as to say that Chocolate advent calendars are the best kind if we want to reinforce this season of expectation. This desire to remember that good stuff is coming but, it is not here quite yet. Let me backpedal a little and confess that I only reached this conclusion in the past few years. My teacher was the Covid pandemic, and the lesson taught to me that waiting for the good stuff to come is worth every second of the process.

During the lockdown, as I live alone, I ate 95% of my meals in isolation and solitude. There were a few sneaky meals shared with the family whose property I rent, as it happens to be in their garden, but apart from that, I mostly ate alone. Everything moved online, including our church service and I developed a deep and fresh appreciation of sharing communion online with my church family. It was the only 'meal' I shared with others during the week. Even during isolation, it became a deep pleasure to share that moment with others. It was a beautiful reminder that although I was alone; I am never alone.

That 'taste' of a meal made me good and hungry to share food with others as soon as it was safe to accomplish. Perhaps the taste of chocolate in the daily Advent calendar is a hint of the good stuff to come in just a few days, or weeks' time. That little treat is enough to make us expectant and ready for the 'adventure' of Advent, that advent, which is, of course, the waiting process itself. A taste is an encouragement. Here is a little bit to get your head and heart ready for the feast to come. Just like the way communion is a foretaste of the feast to come. The feast that will take place in the future, a feast at a table that is continents wide and generations deep.

As you know, we live our lives in the tension of waiting. We are constantly on an adventure; we know the world is not as it should be now. For those of you who are not convinced, five seconds of news is enough to remind us of that fact. Every so often though, we see something, a news item or a social media post that acts like that piece of chocolate. A random act of kindness. Something we experience explicitly reminds us that our world is in the process of redemption. Our waiting, our yearning, our expectation, our peace, and joy anchor themselves in these tiny moments. All that is to say, how can we as humans be a little bit more like those tastes of chocolate in our Advent calendars? How can we enable friends and family to anchor their hopes in the good to come? How can we train ourselves to be patient in our hope and remind those around us that the feast is coming, and it is definitely worth the wait? Also, my favourite Advent chocolate is Cadbury's heroes so how can I be that hero of joy that somebody needs?

*For my non-British readers, The UK had several days of uncertain and constantly changing Christmas plans due to a steep and sudden rise in Covid cases. Different regions of the UK had different rules, as did the devolved nations and they changed as many as four times for people in the week leading up to the 25th of December 2020. People, especially those in the South-East of England, changed groups or tiers every day for four days. This change in rules, meant different limitations on our Christmas celebrations.

Angels

Angels we have heard on high
Sweetly singing o'er the plains,
And the mountains in reply
Echoing their joyous strains.
Shepherds, why this jubilee?
Why your joyous strains prolong?
What the gladsome tidings be
Which inspires your heavenly song?

As a child, I rejected craft. I refused to participate and questioned persistent adults on the educational benefits of such activities. In all honesty, when it came to crafting, I would rather have been reading a book. Which to a high extent is still true today about almost everything. My older brother was far more compliant when it came to crafting. We still have a slightly dodgy looking plaster cast shepherd he created as a young child. He makes his appearance every year. He is fondly referred to as the wandering shepherd and he is my second favourite Christmas ornament in my parent's collection. The first, and ultimate favourite, is a music box. It is the height of 1970's kitsch. The platform is covered in red felt, like a snare drum. On top, stand three blonde-haired blue-eyed angels. Their bodies are made of cones of shiny, pastel paper. Blue, pink, and gold. The gold angel sits atop a Styrofoam ice cube, he does not have a halo, having been lost in a tragic interaction with a toddler's mouth circa 1986. It remains loved. The halo-less angel smiles inanely as the music box plonks out a twinkly, tuneless version of 'Silent Night.' These angels are the toast of my childhood Christmas memories. Although Silent Night is my least favourite carol because they are meant to be joyful, jubilant songs and that one seems to whine on in depression for days. The angels continue to bring a smile to my face even in their dilapidated state.

For a long time, this music box was the only thought I gave to angels in general and their role in the Christmas story. This was until, as a young adult, I moved to one of Britain's most deprived areas. It was quite a violent place and sometimes difficult. Whilst I was there, I started sharing life with some friends, and occasionally babysitting for their young children. Bedtime was my favourite, especially their oldest boy Jack, who was incredibly hilarious and fun.

Jack saw angels and not the kind I would ever wish to meet. He was close to seven years old and was entirely comfortable with the fact that he had seen angels outside his house, protecting him and his family. The young boy described them as sword-wielding, radiant beings who struck holy terror everywhere they went. They were not the slightly odd Barbie dolls that we put on the top of the Christmas tree. These creatures meant business.

The dictionary definition of an angel says, 'an agent or messenger of God.' When we look at this in the context of the Christmas narrative their role seems to be to explain that our protagonists should not be terrified, even though some horrifically terrifying thing is about to take place.

That is how they announced themselves each time in the Christmas story. Let's look at the list for a second:

Do not be afraid, you're thirteen and you're going to have a baby.

Do not be afraid, your fiancée is pregnant.

Do not be afraid, you are going to be the first to see Emmanuel.

Do not be afraid, you need to flee your homeland to protect your child.

Cast your mind back to the beginning of the pandemic, and consider what the angels, the sword-wielding messenger, might have said to you:

Do not be afraid, you are going to be separated from your loved ones.

Do not be afraid, your way of life is going to be drastically altered.

Do not be afraid, home-schooling for six months is awesome! No really, it is, and Joe Wicks will help you.

Do not be afraid, you are going to be unemployed.

I guess we would have run a mile; questioned God, and found ourselves meditating, even fixated, on the end of those sentences, not the beginning.

But that is the main issue, with angels in the Christmas story. That is the only thing we see them perform in the Christmas story. Herald a terrifying event and announce not to fear, then disappear without so much as a tinsel halo as a reminder. This makes me wonder, is much of what they do unseen? Does the phrase do not be afraid insinuate something? Does it suggest that angels are working behind the scenes on your behalf? At the end of the most disruptive eighteen months of my life, I must believe in this reality. Angelic things have happened in this pandemic season. Moments, where it appeared that all was lost, have been at least slightly rectified by surprise deliveries of flowers, brownies, and vegetable samosas. The latter arrived on a Saturday evening in early February when I had attended three zoom funerals, on two different continents, within forty-eight hours. Surprise phone calls and encouraging notes have whispered to me, and to others, not to be afraid. As have majestic sunrises, and cool breezes on hot days. The delight of watching a group of foxes' dances in the moonlight was angelic. The dazzling light may well have been the security light on the workshop, but that is far less romantic.

The angels appear in the story with news, and the exhortation to not be afraid and then right at the end of the narrative, their interaction with the shepherds they announce:

'Peace on Earth and goodwill toward men.'

With everything I see in our world at the moment, I cannot say with certainty that we have achieved this promise. There in the busyness of the Christmas season; there is little peace, and in a pressure moment, zero goodwill. Is it because we are afraid? Afraid that our preparations will not be good enough? Afraid that the gift we have searched out and purchased will be rejected? Afraid of the nagging void that we numb with behaviours and busyness will refuse to be silenced? Are we afraid that if we stop, and get off the hamster wheel of frenetic activity, someone else might be hurt? To a greater or lesser extent, I think these observations are all true, about all of us some of the time.

The angels in this story ask us to raise our eyes outside of ourselves. The angles invite us to see the vast beauty of the night sky. They invite us to remember that the limits of space are but a single handspan of the eternal author. If we see ourselves in the light of those dimensions, our failure to reach perfection in our Christmas preparations disappears. Perhaps our fear of other people and losing our life will dissipate as well. As those fears subside, in its place arrives a desire to spread goodwill and peace to all men.

We have such a short amount of time, that to consider anything more important than the creation of peace, or the imagination of justice denies or decreases our humanity. Therefore, these angels who tell us not to be afraid, also remind us of our inconsequential and fragile nature. Thankfully, they do not leave us there and their angelically inspired human counterparts, I am talking about you my friends, remind us others are working on our behalf. Finally, they provide us with an opportunity to realise the finite nature of our lives. Beyond that, there is an invitation for us to understand and participate in peace and goodwill for all men. These steps are both beautiful and inevitable. The more you realise you are finite, the more willing you are to be angelic and take steps to remind people not to be afraid. This spreads goodwill and peace.

The angels remind us that whatever terrifying messages they may bring to us, there will be others working on our behalf. These will be in both seen and unseen ways. Beyond that, the message of the angels invites us to see our story on the backdrop of eternity. The comfort that this challenge, ahead of us, whatever it may be, will eventually be a sentence in our story and a pinprick of a star on the vast darkness of eternity is such a comfort. They also whisper, most importantly amid our distresses, you are not alone.

Beyond that, practical ways that communities have taken care of each other, during the pandemic, and the delight of nature in moments of despair, angels can seem aloof.

As we look for angels as a sign of the arrival of Christmas, let us take a minute and remember to stay in the first part of the sentence. And whatever the new year brings, do not be afraid.

Songs

'Oh, there's no place like home for the holidays,
Cause no matter how far away you roam,
When you pine for the sunshine of a friendly gaze,
For the holidays, you can't beat home sweet home.

I used to live in the midwestern United States. The flyover ones. Tricky to manoeuvre in and out of at the best of times. In December, with the unpredictable weather, it gets even more complicated. One year, I decided to stay in the Midwest for the Christmas season. As I did that, the friends I considered family decided to travel, for the first time in years. I was facing Christmas alone. It did not end up that way, but for a few hours, I wished I was home, and tapping my together feet a la Judy Garland in the classic movie 'The Wizard of Oz, left me firmly in Missouri. As I turned on the engine, in my car, ubiquitous in nature, the Christmas music station chose this very moment to play the song; 'There's No Place Like Home for the Holidays.' It is a slice of Americana. It is played constantly from Thanksgiving to New Year and Perry Como's silky tones sing out.

'Oh, there's no place like home for the holidays,
Cause no matter how far away you roam,
When you pine for the sunshine of a friendly gaze,
For the holidays, you can't beat home sweet home.'

I sat in my car and a little tear dribbled down my cheek. Songs transport us like nothing else I have experienced. At that moment, emotionally, it was so evocative, that I was home. Not just home as a generic place; but home. To my dad's wry smile at whatever absurd situation was in front of us. The memory of that smile calmed my soul. The song reminded me that whatever happened I could find my way home and that smile would be waiting.

Until it wasn't. My dad passed away in the late autumn of 2012 and suddenly home would never be complete again. Something was changed in my family, and it couldn't be replaced. Home in that sense became a memory. As Autumn dissolved into winter that year, other songs transported me. Often my soul was shaped in a different way, away from peace into a grief that seemed to deepen as the pressure to be cheerful, that we sometimes find ourselves in, during December, increased and left me exhausted. There are lots of phrases and memes to drag us out of this place. There is the one about friends being the ones who remind us of our heart's song when we have forgotten. There is also the one about speaking the truth even when our voice shakes. For some reason, something in that phrase deeply resonated with my soul. When our voice shakes, it is because everything has been shaken within us, and the foundations we knew, have shifted to the newer, but the truer ground. Often, we have a binary way of thinking about songs. This fact is especially true when our feelings about life are extreme, we look for songs to express our feelings. Love songs that shout I'm on top of the world.' 'Always and Forever.' When life is not going in our favour, we look for songs that express our hurt. People have become millionaires singing songs that we flock to when we need to get our feelings out or when we need to process our feelings.

The Christmas songs that we sing root themselves in our positive emotions. The carols we sing are expressions of those emotions. However, when our lives are not in that place, when our feelings and therefore, our voices shake. The truth remains. As we sing them their truth, and perhaps our participation in that truth through singing, shapes our emotions. My voice and my personality were definitely shaky as I entered the church for the Christmas Carol service in December 2012. Familiar faces smiled those pathetic, 'I do not know what to say to you smiles.' I wanted to be invisible.

33

Familiar readings followed and it all felt very untrue. Life had been hard, and my faith was shaken. My voice trembled as a reflection of the disruption to my faith. The songs told the story, but where there was, in everyone else, an expression of joy, for me there was a desperate cry for connection. I needed those truths to shape my feelings. I needed to know that at some point, everything would not feel like hopeless bullshit. It was not until the final Christmas Carol that I experienced the transformative nature of these truths.

We were singing 'Oh Little Town of Bethlehem.' the last verse says this:

O holy Child of Bethlehem
Descend to us, we pray
Cast out our sin and enter in
Be born to us today
We hear the Christmas angels
The great glad tidings tell
O come to us, abide with us
Our Lord Emmanuel
O come to us, abide with us
Our Lord Emmanuel

At that moment, those verses, sung with shaky unintentional vibrato, shaped my soul. An invitation to the Everlasting Father to live with me inside my grief and inhabit that space together. I realised at that moment that my sadness was Holy to Him. He loved me enough to remind me that whilst my experience of home had been altered forever in His house I would never be lost. Whatever grief or joy I held, there was a space at a table where I would always be welcome no matter the state of my soul.

The words of those carols are incredibly familiar. Perhaps, in my state, I needed something familiar so that my brain could get out of the way long enough for my soul to be transported. I am not sure what happened at that moment, but it made the possibility of my grief shifting seem real.

The familiarity of both word and tune lowered my guard and I was shaped by the powerful invitation to abide. Abide means to rest and discover one's true self within something. Isn't that the most beautiful idea? The best songs, be they Perry Como's American hits, or the Victorian carols of our ancestors, invite us to abide and find ourselves inside their lyrics.

I was recently reunited with my first carol piano book from my childhood. I can remember receiving it when I was about eight years old. I was excited to be playing music that I knew. Songs I could recognise, after the endless scales and exercises of an elementary piano student. My excitement lasted about ten minutes after I got home. The words and melodies were so familiar to me. I could see what my right hand was supposed to play; I could hear how the tune was supposed to sound. But putting those together, with the chords and bass of the left hand and the more than 'just the melody' in the right hand' still took practice.

My childhood brain was somewhere between disappointed and agitated because something so familiar was also so complex. There were so many more elements, than my childhood experience, of singing the melody to 'Away in a Manger' a thousand times.

Isn't that also true of the Christmas story? For that is what we sing in these carols and hymns, the Christmas story. There are words that we sing each Christmas that are so familiar. Many of us have them memorized without knowing. We sing them without thinking and our familiarity has bred a little contempt and lost a little wonder. I mean think about these phrases taken from carols we sing each year.

'Veiled in flesh The Godhead see
Hail the incarnate deity
Pleased as man, with man to dwell
Jesus our Emmanuel.'

'No more let sins and sorrows grow
Nor thorns infest the ground
He comes to make His blessings flow
Far as the curse is found.

These are a little more complex than Baa baa black sheep are they not? We seem to sing them with gusto each year. In our exuberance and excitement, I think we forget the depth and mystery and wonder.

There was one song that I was not familiar with contained in the book 'Oh Holy Night'. I never learned to play it, but I loved the power of the words, even as a small child. I do not remember even hearing it performed live growing up, but it was ubiquitous in the states, and friends and I would joke about the million times we would hear it starting in early November. It was originally banned because of the subversive nature of its lyrics in a society that still contained slavery. A phrase like 'Bonds, he will break; because the slave is our brother.' packs some punch. Churches also banned it because the author of the poem was an avowed atheist proving once again that God can use anyone to rattle some cages. Its powerful lyrics remind us that the songs of the church are meant to be subversive, and we miss the point of the Gospel if we do not see a way that it can transform us into a more just society. We cannot claim 'Oh Holy Night.' If we are not prepared to work to break the binds of injustice for our fellow man.

Singing is subversive. Singing is vital. It gives life and expresses something of a connection between body and voice. No, more than that, a connection between body and soul, between souls and spirits. The song, and the act of singing, are part of eternity. During the strange Covid year I sang alone, through tears, through grief and loss. I sang to remind myself that I had not always felt numb. I am no great singer, but it gives air to my emotions when I sing.

During the strange year of Covid at one of the least restricted times when meeting up was allowed but singing was not, a friend and I sat back-to-back in her hot tub, blared some tunes, and sang. It felt subversive, the way singing should be experienced.

Carol singing is subversive! The word carol literally means to sing and dance in a circle. The tradition of going house to house singing carols developed because of the exuberance with which these songs were sung throughout history. It is true. In the Middle Ages, churches found the explosive joy with which people sang these Christmas songs disrupted their church services and the solemnity of the mass. To avoid this kind of celebration disrupting the status quo they banned Christmas Carols and dancing, The carol singers simply left;

they took their joy and delight out into the market square and began to go door to door. As they went, they sang and danced with joy. They invited the community to join in their subversive joy. They sang an invitation to join their ancient song. The song said to those in the village there is a place for you in our community of exiles. As we sing these stories each December with our cups of mulled wine and our slightly dodgy descants, we invite others to find their place in a song that has echoed since time began.

Some friends of mine have a cookie and carol party each year. They live in a Cul-de-Sac and ninety per cent of the close crowd together at the bottom to sing carols and eat cookies. The festival is inclusive. The Hindu neighbours join in each year, my personal highlight of the event is drinking my mulled wine with one of their vegetable samosas whilst trying to do the harmony for Hark the Herald Angels sing. Few of these revellers attend church regularly, but in these sacred songs that they sing with gusto, there is an ancient invitation. I love the special music of Christmas, the transcendence of beautiful harmonies and excellent musicianship; but I also love these messy subversive expressions of Christmas and community. I think there is space for both, and I think there is space for everything in between. Sing with your shaky soul this winter, sing full of joy and hope, and remind others of their place in the song, especially if it seems their soul has forgotten.

Trees

The Holly and the Ivy,
When they are both full grown,
Of all the trees that are in the wood,
The Holly bears the crown.

In my mid-twenties, I was doing the roommate thing. It's a strange age, starting to establish yourself as an adult, creating our traditions and expressions of life as an adult. My roommate and I had a tradition of decorating the tree and then eating Indian food and watching 'It's A Wonderful Life.' The other tradition was, a slightly less celebratory one, neither of us grew up in St. Louis, the city where we lived. Therefore, Christmas visits to family would mean leaving around December 20th. Due to the distance, for both of us, we would be gone until well into the new year. We were devotees to the real tree, and master procrastinators, who wants to spend their precious free time taking a Christmas tree down. On top of all that, our apartment complex had posted signs... no Christmas trees in the dumpsters. This removed the possibility of the tree coming down even further. It was Valentine's Day when we finally reached the point where we could no longer stand the tree in the apartment and the night came. Under the cover of darkness, we took the tree to the dumpster. There was a convincing trail of pine needles leading from our front door, down three flights of stairs and across the courtyard. We spent the rest of the evening trying to spread the pine needles across our neighbour's doors so that we could at least prove that the tree procrastinators existed in abundance.

I remember this moment because it put me off having a tree for years, it just seemed like so much hassle. It did not seem to mean anything and my desire not to get in trouble with my illegal tree dumping was challenging. When I began the research for this little book, I had a perceived narrative from British culture that the origin of the Christmas tree in our family homes is Victorian and possibly under our Germanic influence. This narrative is true for the family Christmas tree that we adorn each December. The one that is the perfectionists' nemesis as they attempt to get the ornaments perfectly aligned. The toddlers' dream as bright and shiny baubles are placed within their reach. The one that sparks the eternal debate over real or fake.

The one that we cover with lights and adorn with memories. The individual tree does find its origins in Germany, but there are accounts of Christmas trees in villages, towns and cities as early as the 1200s.

Yes, you read that correctly, the 1200s. Long before the marketing machines that throws Christmas at us each year existed trees and decorations were homemade and packed with meaning. These trees were decorated simply. They typically had only two decorations, on their branches, Apples and Candles. Now obviously, this is in part due to the availability of plastic baubles and Mickey Mouse ears in medieval England. However, the decorations had value and meaning for the community. They were placed intentionally by the community whose lives very much centred around the rhythms of the church. The entire village shared one tree, placed in the centre of the nave of the village church.

The tree would have been placed in the church at the beginning of December. The start of Advent. Up until the early part of the twentieth century, Advent was a solemn season similar to Lent, and many people would fast or refrain from treats to remind themselves of the depth of their longing. The story of Christmas starts long before 0BC. Historically, people took time to commemorate this waiting. We seem to skip Advent as a season of longing and once the first door of the calendar is open, and sometimes before, we don our Santa hats and sweaters and start the party. It was not always that way. It began with the placing of the tree, representative of the tree in the first garden, the tree that made waiting for a saviour a necessity in first place. A reminder that there was a plan all the time, and that this season of longing was not futile. For our medieval ancestors, the tree epitomised the sense of longing, for it was a tree that started the need for Christmas in the story of redemptive history.

This communal village tree would have been a visual reminder of the tree in the garden where Adam and Eve started their lives. The apples are a reminder of the fruit that fuelled the need for the saviour. Our modern celebrations seem to start with 90% of the story told. We have cut ourselves off from this sense of waiting, instant gratification, and celebration but our medieval ancestors started at the beginning a very good place to start and I believe their celebrations were richer for that philosophy.

I love this idea of remembering the beginning. It makes the story richer. It reminds us that we are not the entire story, that we are part of a continuum. We are part of a family that is continents wide and generations deep. We do not exist in isolation and neither does our story. The tree was that visual reminder of where the story came from, and the longing for home that we all feel is much bigger than wanting the perfect Christmas and the perfect tree. As we remember the beginning, we are reminded that perfection does not exist. It reminds us that as the needles of the pine tree begin to fall, during that cold part of December when it never seems to get fully into daylight, something else begins to live.

The analogy of the tree gets better. It really does. The ancient church had many feast days of significance and historically, December 24th was the feast of Adam and Eve. It is interesting that this festival was so close to the celebration of the arrival of the second Adam. The Son of Man who came to defeat the works of darkness; the darkness that entered the world through the disobedience of the first Adam.

The apples would have been on the tree since the beginning of December, but the candles were added slowly week by week during Advent. They would have been lighted on the tree during the mass to celebrate the feast of Adam and Eve. A sign that as we remember those first humans, we also remember the light that shines in the darkness.

At the end of the mass, the tree would be taken from the church in a procession of light. When the congregation reached the town square, the carollers would sing and dance in a joyous celebration and the tree would be burned. The entire village would gather, and in the style of stone soup, bring something for the village to share. Can you see the complete meaning and story of the Gospel here? The focal point of the celebration, in the dark northern climes of a British December, without the light pollution of the twenty-first century, was the ceremonial burning of the Christmas tree. The tree was burned to light up the night. To hail the arrival of the light of the world. It was a profound act of communion as we celebrate the arrival of Jesus and it was no mistake that the entire village would cook their feast on this burning tree and through sharing the entire village would be fed, and if the historians were to be believed would have been fed a feast that makes our family Christmas lunches look tiny by comparison.

A tree had to die so that something else could live. I have been struck by that idea. We kill something so that something else can live. What else in this disrupted, distorted, and sometimes devastating past few years, have I had to kill off, and what things have lived because of it?

I have killed off expectation so that being at peace with reality has a chance to live.

Killed off perfectionism, or at least I am trying to, so that progress can be celebrated.

Killed media consumption, so that creativity has a chance to live.

Killed time with family, so that other people can live.

One of the things I have noticed as I have been thinking through these Christmas traditions of our ancestors is that they did not separate Christmas and Easter. In their minds, they were part of the same celebration so this destruction of the tree was linked to the tree that caused death so that we could all live forever. Researching and writing this little book has cured me of my tree lethargy and apathy. I will buy a tree this year and cover it in apples and lights. I will remember the tree that started the story and the light of the world that completed its work. I will also ceremoniously burn it on Christmas Eve and invite all those who are without a tree to come and feast on its bounty, to contribute anything they can to our celebration. We will also warm our hands and perhaps souls on the warmth its destruction provides. Perhaps we will find ourselves caught up in that ancient story in a new way.

Our journey from communal to individual seems to have started with the industrial revolution. The enlightenment did prioritise the individual over the collective; therefore, it seems natural that our celebrations followed that same story. However, there are still acts of generosity and peace-making connected with the tradition, acts that have lasted into the hyper-individualistic age in which we exist. The tree in Trafalgar Square is a gift from the Norwegian people. The tradition started in 1947 as a thank you for the support and cooperation of the British people during the second world war. In those post-war years, few British people prioritised trees at Christmas. The tree in Rockefeller Centre is older than the tree in Trafalgar Square. This tradition started in 1931, during the depression era construction of the Centre when few in New York could afford their own tree, the communal tree had a chance to live again. Parents would bring children to see the tree at the Rockefeller Centre or in Trafalgar Square as their Christmas treat. It seems as we become more affluent, we become more individualistic, and in our times of collective need, we lean into a community to fill in the gaps. These gaps are perhaps acutely felt by those whom our misplaced need to be self-sufficient leaves behind. This idea, albeit an ancient one of a singular communal tree, in the central point of a community, could be the leveller our society needs as we emerge from the pandemic, more aware than ever of our need for each other and real community.

For in those moments after the depression and in post-war London everyone needed some joy. A lighted tree is a source of delight. I do not care how old you are. In those contexts, many of the people delighted to see a tree, could not afford such a personal extravagance. Those on the up and those who had fallen a long way brought their families to see the big central tree. You may have been there with a person who was a million dollars poorer than they were before the Wall Street Crash or a million dollars richer, but in the great equalizer of experiences over things the view is the same In the darkness of the December evening, the cut of your coat or the patch on your trousers would be invisible, and even if it were not, the tree is the main event here, not your clothes. The delight for your family would be solely based on your capacity for joy and gratitude.

As personal affluence increased again, convenience and personal privacy became of higher value. These three factors most certainly contributed to the fact that trees and much of our celebrations of Christmas moved inside. When this happens, everyone misses out. The opportunity of watching someone else find delight in something disappears. When fewer people share our experiences, this decrease is automatic. If we can pay attention for long enough to realise what has happened as we have a voyeuristic observation of someone else's joy. This voyeuristic tendency in the human psyche is why people-watching is so exhilarating. After a long day, and a difficult season, post-war Londoners visited the tree in Trafalgar Square. They found there a sense of satisfaction, after a long and brutal war to see something beautiful and extravagant in its generosity. There was also joy at the satisfaction of delight of others. Those present had lived through the blitz, rationing and the horrors of war together they shared this moment of delight and wonder. I have no proof of this beyond anecdotal stories from long-deceased relatives, but I am convinced that this shared moment would have been intensified because of the journey that they took to reach that point. Just think about that first

46

pint or cocktail you shared with a friend post lockdown. The moment was sweeter and the pint tastier because of the journey you had taken to reach that point, even if you did have to wear a mask when you went to the toilet.

As I write it is late Summer 2021 and we are hopefully journeying away from the pandemic that has disrupted our lives for the past year and a half. The pandemic has been a shared experience that has helped us see what is important in our lives and highlighted what is missing and essential in our communities. If we are allowed to have big celebrations this Winter, I am going to visit the tree in Trafalgar Square with friends and family. On top of that, in a most Non-British way, I am going to make eye contact with a stranger who is visiting at the same time. We will share a knowing smile and I may be so bold as to ask them why they came, and what they are hoping to achieve or experience through their visit. Christmas trees are levellers, they have been levellers since the Middle Ages. The delight they have caused through the years has of course only multiplied in the sharing.

Gifts

Born a King on Bethlehem's plain,
Gold I bring to crown him again
King forever, ceasing never
Over us all to reign.

Myrrh is mine: Its bitter perfume
Breathes a life of gathering gloom.
Sorrowing, sighing, bleeding dying,
Sealed in the stone-cold tomb.

Frankincense to offer have I.
Incense owns a Deity nigh.
Prayer and praising all men raising,
Worship Him, God on high.

Ask any child their favourite part of the Christmas season and you will largely receive the same answer. PRESENTS. It can be exhilarating to receive a gift, especially when the contents are a surprise or when someone hits on the exact thing that you wanted. Better yet if you did not know that you wanted it, until you opened the present. I have a couple of friends that have this gift. They seem to have this extra sense and effortlessly know what to purchase. The gifts we receive from these friends, somehow makes us feel known and seen. For the rest of us, myself included, gift purchasing can be a chore! The stores and shops are crowded, noisy affairs and the queues are long. Everything on sale is trying to grab my attention and seems to kill my inspiration.

The challenge is that we need so little. Our houses, our bathrooms, bedrooms, and bellies are full. Many of us have storage lockers full of the things that we might need one day but do not have space for in our homes. The popularity of Marie Kondo and The Minimalists provide us with the answer. We have too much stuff. This problem is not new. When Mary and Joseph arrived in Bethlehem the houses, hostels and guest houses were full. There was no room at the Inn for the greatest gift that was ever given to humanity. The season of Advent is a season for making room. As I said earlier, we make space in our bellies through fasting for a period of feasting. Perhaps, we could also take some time to make space in our homes by purging ourselves of things we no longer need, put into regular use, or require. There have been suggestions from all over the place about donating to charity one item on December 1st and two on December second and so on. By Christmas Eve, we would have removed 270 items from our homes. Before you, all freak-out, and scream that there would be nothing left, the average family home with two adults and two children contains a staggering 400,000 items. 300,000 of which we do not use on a regular basis. By going through this process of an Advent Spring cleaning of sorts we will be able to see how much more we actually possess. Dietrich Bonhoffer said this

'I think we're going to have an exceptionally good Christmas. The very fact that every outward circumstance precludes our making provision for it will show whether we can be content with what is truly essential. I used to be very fond of thinking up and buying presents, but now that we have nothing to give, the gift God gave us in the birth of Christ will seem all the more glorious; the emptier our hands, the better we understand what Luther meant by his dying words 'We're beggars; it's true." The poorer our quarters, the more clearly, we perceive that our hearts should be Christ's home on earth.'

What is most remarkable about this statement is not just the profound simplicity of its prose. The most astonishing fact is that this letter was written in 1943 to his fiancée. At this time, Bonhoeffer was in a Nazi prison awaiting execution for a failed assassination attempt on Hitler.

It is true the less we have, the more clearly, we can see what we actually possess. If we go through a purge in the days of Advent, when Christmas day arrives, we will have space in our homes to receive the gifts that make us feel seen and known. We may also find ourselves with space in our hearts to see the real gifts around us in a new way. If we learnt anything from our Covid Christmas it was that we preferred presence over presents.

51

Everything that we possess requires energy. To keep it orderly and clean. To appreciate something, you need space around it to be able to see the item and its value. If we own less, we will be better able to see and therefore appreciate the gifts we receive and their value.

A few years ago, a group of families I know took this seriously one Christmas. They decided to trial a four-gift philosophy for their children.

1. Something they wanted
2. Something they needed
3. Something to wear
4. Something to read

I was a big fan of the last one and gave many age-appropriate book recommendations. In the Facebook group, there were many discussions around the thing they needed. Many of the families identified through this process that their children, and indeed themselves, needed nothing. A sure-fire sign that we are heading in the right direction if we take on an Advent challenge to make more room. If you can't identify something they need, you could always reduce the number of gifts to three, after all, Jesus received three gifts.

Before you peg me as a Grinch-like character, who wants to rid your home of Christmas joy; I really must confess something. I am pretty good at being ruthless with possessions, except books and gifts. I still have many handmade and questionable gifts from my teaching days. I appreciate the effort exhausted parents put into creating each item. Sometimes, they even let the children help. Gifts of any kind let us know that we are seen as a person, but there is something about a handmade gift, from a child, that fills the giver with unspeakable joy. This is a further paradox in the conundrum of gift-giving. The delight of giving gifts is really in the giving: but in order for that to happen, we must have people to receive the gifts. Perhaps the future is in donating to charities on other's behalf. Helping them feel seen by actually helping others. Or the gift of an experience, that comes with your presence, outside of the Christmas season. Tickets to a show or a baking class or the cinema. The winter is so long. Who wouldn't love a little pick me up to look forward to in the dull months of January and February? Something unique to the person who is in front of you, that they do not have to clean and store. This gift will help them see what they have in your relationship or friendship.

The gifts the travelling stargazers brought to Jesus perform exactly that function. Their gifts brought with them an affirmation of all that the Baby Jesus would become in life. It whispered to us, all that we have in our relationship with Him. Maybe this is repetition for you, but the gold represented His status as King. The myrrh is an embalming oil, a symbol therefore of death. His death of course, but also the beginning of the death of every bad thing. Finally, Frankincense, which sounds like a cheap cologne, speaks of the priestly nature of Jesus. In the Old Testament, Frankincense was used to represent the presence of God. So, in bringing Frankincense to Jesus, it is a reminder or a sign of the beginning of Emmanuel - God with us.

Gifts with purpose, gifts that call out to something unique or precious that you have seen in the person who is receiving the gift is not a new idea. The greatest author of the twentieth century, CS Lewis, demonstrates this idea to us in the Chronicles of Narnia. Where, after a hundred years of winter, but never Christmas, the day is finally arriving and the sounds of sleighs with bells can be heard in the land. A solemn Father Christmas gives the children, swords, bows, a horn and a potion that brings healing. All things that throughout the proceeding story the children need to fulfil the tasks ahead of them. Another favourite author of mine this time from the 18th century, Victor Hugo, started a Christmas celebration for impoverished children on the Island of Guernsey. They came into his home, shared a meal, and received presents. This is what he said in a letter to his Father-in-law about the experience, and the solemn advice he gave to the children.

My dear children, amongst the toys I have just given you, you will find no guns, no cannon, or swords, no murderous weapon that would make you think of war and destruction. War is a dreadful thing; the people of this world are made for loving one another, not killing each other. The girls will find dolls to play with, ideal for learning how to be mother, which will be their job later in life. For the boys there are little boats and little trains, in other words toys designed to encourage work, progress and the mind, and not destruction.

Of course, time has shifted on, and I hope today we would be equally comfortable giving a boy a doll and a girl a little boat, but the heart behind it is that we call something out in the young people in our lives something that perhaps projects them to a leap forward in progress and develops their mind and heart toward justice.

What might this look like in the 21st century? Well, I had an aunt who gave me a charm each year for a bracelet, they are a living history of my childhood as they often spoke of my interests during the preceding year. They were monuments of the life I had lived; but also, thoughtful gifts that propelled me to my interests and character. I still have the bracelet and occasionally look at the charms and remember the person I was and the one my aunt helped me become.

Perhaps this is where we should be heading with our gift-giving, particularly with the children in our lives. Let us call out something aspirational or affirmational in them through our gift-giving and then let us see what impact our meaningful gifts have on the next generation as we move away from the mayhem of Christmas shopping toward the idea of a simplified gift exchange that prioritises presence over presents.

Nativity Play

Whenever I see girls and boys
Selling lanterns on the street
I remember the child in the manger as he sleeps
Wherever there are people
Giving gifts exchanging cards
I believe that Christmas is truly in their hearts
Let's light our Christmas trees for a bright tomorrow
Where nations are at peace,
And all are one in God.

We all like to leave parts out of our stories, we like to sanitize the gritty bits of our lives. The bits that make us vulnerable, ashamed, desperate to forget. It can get lonely as we trade our authenticity for socially acceptable versions of ourselves. We also do this with the Christmas story. Most people find the narrative of baby Jesus meek and mild acceptable. I mean Talladega Nights says it all. '8lb Baby Jesus will help us.' But even in the predictions of his birth, there are signs of his radical, subversive, and world-changing nature. It drives me nuts, because we leave them out, every year. Our community needs these parts of the story. Let's look for a second at one of the most edited portions of the Christmas narrative contained within the Bible in the book of Isaiah. The story typically starts at verse 2

Nevertheless, there will be no more gloom for those who were in distress. In the past, he humbled the land of Zebulun and the land of Naphtali, but in the future, he will honour Galilee of the nations, by the Way of the Sea, beyond the Jordan—
² The people walking in darkness
*   have seen a great light;*
on those living in the land of deep darkness
*   a light has dawned.*

Often the narrative stops here. The church is full, the candles are twinkling, and we are excited about the light that shines in the darkness. Sometimes, the narrative jumps to verse 6:

⁶ For to us a child is born,
*   to us, a son is given,*
*   and the government will be on his shoulders.*
And he will be called
*   Wonderful Counsellor, Mighty God,*

58

Everlasting Father, Prince of Peace.
[7] Of the greatness of his government and peace
there will be no end.

Again, this is truth, the light, the titles they fill us with hope.
We feel good and we smile. But we have missed the
dangerous bit of the story, the crisis and the climax. We have
skipped from the Balance of Baby Jesus to the New Balance of
the world at rights. WE DO NOT LIVE THERE! We have missed
this bit:

[3] You have enlarged the nation
and increased their joy;

The gospel is bigger than any nationality or grouping or
previous tribe. There is room for everyone!

they rejoice before you as people rejoice at the harvest,
as warriors rejoice when dividing the plunder.
[4] For as in the day of Midian's defeat, you have shattered the
yoke that burdens them, the bar across their shoulders, the
rod of their oppressor.
[5] Every warrior's boot used in battle and every garment rolled
in blood will be destined for burning, will be fuel for the fire.

I am going to say this only once, I have no space in my
understanding of the Christmas story that does not remove
oppression from all people. I am a challenger at heart, and I
want to say to you, dear reader, that when you break
oppression, of any kind, you take your place in the Christmas
story. I am beginning to think that perhaps our Scandinavian
friends have this correct. They refer to the Christmas season
as 'jul.' The origin of that word is 'revolution.' So, when they

wish you a 'good jul,' they are wishing you a good revolution. I think this statement, is perhaps the most accurate description of Jesus' mission on earth. A revolution of good, for good, forever. It acknowledges His power, majesty, and vulnerability. His message and His destiny. The beginning of the end of every bad thing. It is only when we acknowledge the gritty bits, the revolutionary nature of Jesus that we have any hope of reaching these final wonderful verses and the promises they contain:

6 For to us a child is born,
   to us, a son is given,
   and the government will be on his shoulders.
And he will be called
   Wonderful Counselor, Mighty God,
   Everlasting Father, Prince of Peace.
7 Of the greatness of his government and peace
   there will be no end.
He will reign on David's throne
   and over his kingdom,
establishing and upholding it
   with justice and righteousness
   from that time on and forever.
The zeal of the LORD Almighty
   will accomplish this.

There are some parts of the Christmas story that are 18 rated. Medieval tradition celebrated the feast of the Holy Innocents on December 28th. One boy would be appointed Bishop for the day, it is unclear what responsibilities and privileges he possessed; however, no one would volunteer for the position. It is said that all the other boys in the village would have been savagely beaten in the square, to remind the villagers of the murders of the young boys under the reign of Herod and to foster gratitude in the boys that they were not alive at the time of Jesus and thus murdered. Nothing inspires gratitude quite like a savage beating, right? It seems that the Church has managed to get things wrong throughout history and perhaps this was the only time in church history when it was better to be a girl than a boy. There is part of this tradition that grotesquely intrigues me, it fosters participation from a young age. Participation in a story that is bigger than themselves. The public flogging can be dispensed with, but participation is a necessary part of fostering community and that's why even though I was always the narrator, I love the nativity play at schools and churches each Christmas.

My parents breathed a sigh of relief; my memory is that my narrator costume was my school uniform. I never voiced my consternation or disappointment, that would be very un-British of me, but I wanted to be in the story. I wanted to show and not tell. Perhaps, in the donning of a costume, in my childish head, there was a sense of identification that I could say that the story was mine. MINE. There is a moment of terror for families each year as the holy chaos of casting and therefore, costuming is announced. It's one of my favourite scenes in the Christmas classic, definitely not for children, Love Actually:

Kid: Guess, what I am going to be in the school play Mummy?
Mum: Mary, an angel?
Kid: A lobster, the second one.
Mum: There was more than one lobster present at the birth of Christ?

Then the scene slips forward, in the interconnected nature of the narrative, where we see the distraught mother putting the final touches on the papier-mache lobster head. This mother has invested hours, of her busy December, into the creation of this costume. Why? Participation, the child in this film, memorizes the story, albeit a slightly odd one with the additional, extra-Biblical creatures. The child then participates in the retelling of this ancient story. Maybe it stirs in you a memory of a time when you told the story or a time that you realised the story was true. That in fact, even in the slightly odd narratives that include multiple lobsters, they might discover that the story is also theirs to possess and to share.

Frederick Buechner in his book Telling Secrets says this bite sized piece of wisdom:

'My story is important, not because it is mine, goodness no, but if I tell it anywhere near properly, you will see that it is also yours.'

I believe this statement is true for your children as they learn to tell the story of the nativity. They are aware of the hierarchy of participation as well. My young cousin aged four made this comment at the conclusion of her first nativity play

'This year I was an angel and that's fine; next year, I'm being Mary.' The story was hers and the role she played, she played well; and now she is hungry to increase her participation and connection to this story that is continents wide and generations deep.

So, weary parents, painting a lobster head or creating a tinsel halo, hours after the children are in bed. If you're exhausted at the idea of building a crib with power tools that would not have been invented for almost two thousand years. Take a deep breath as you apply that make-up or search for an unstained dishcloth for a shepherd's headdress. Pause and contain your frustration as your seven-year-old learns lines with you and says Frankenstein not Frankincense for the seven hundredth time. You are not alone as you are wondering whether it is worth it as you fix a sheep's ear or wonder what the point is when that annoying song they have been singing, for what seems like decades, is now keeping you awake, as it spins in your head among the terrifying list of things you must do tomorrow. You are offering more than a homemade costume and a chance to shine. You are hiding a story in their hearts that has influenced communities for centuries, and if they participate well, it might just offer them the healing they need in the re-telling later.

I will tell you this next story because it is mine, and if I tell it well enough you might see that it is also yours. My narrator days were long behind me. I had grown and flown and returned and failed. Life had been very difficult for a few months, and I had been on automatic pilot, doing the bare minimum to survive. Discovering who I was before anyone told me what I should become. Emotionally, I felt like a young toddler, just starting to walk, wobbling all over the place and unsure of what I could achieve.

I joined a community group that was getting ready for the Christmas season. We began to plan Christmas parties, services, and events. We talked about living and sharing life together and shared our stories. I became comfortable with saying the phrase 'I am unemployed.' quite often as people asked what I did and other invasive questions. It was a little strange when I think about it, but I was growing accustomed to feeling a little strange. We started one evening to talk about the children's nativity service and various members of the group expressed their disappointment at the cheesiness of the scripts that were available to buy. I am the epitome of an internal processor; I prefer to think things through before I speak to them out loud. There was much going on inside my brain and so I blurted out:

'I can write a play, how about a rhyming one in the style of Dr Seuss?'

Everyone jumped on the idea, and I walked out of the room that evening with three weeks to write a play. I was not entirely sure what had happened, and I felt like I had about the same concentration span and ability to stick to a structure at my disposal as the wobbly toddler. I climbed into bed that evening full of no ideas, and no clue where to start. In the middle of the night, I sat bolt upright, sleepily I turned on the light and imagined a large group of angels, all shouting this phrase:

Glory to God, heaven and earth reunited, the whole of creation is growing excited.

It was a start, a phrase, a moment to aim towards in the story arc. I wrote it out twice on my post-it note:

Glory to God, heaven and earth reunited; the whole of creation is growing excited.

Glory to God, heaven and earth reunited; the whole of creation is growing excited.

And in that phrase, that became a scene, that became a full script, that became a lot of hours painting brightly coloured backdrops on damp floors, is all the truth about the story of the nativity, you will ever need. It was simply the beginning of the end of every bad thing. It began something in me as well, I participated in that story in a new way that year. I had been through it over the past eleven months, finding a new way to tell that story, rekindling in me a memory of a time when there was joy. I may never have been more than a narrator, but telling that story every year, participating in its ancient truths, started something in me, that when the time was right brought a healing and restoration of my creativity that I have developed and relied upon ever since. I had to reckon with some of the gritty parts of my story as I wrote that play and it wasn't until I reached the final lines of the play that I realised how deep the connection between this story and my own journey had been over that previous year. The final lines of the play say this:

From different routes, the visitors came
to see the lad of Christmas Fame.
I want to say I'm glad you came,
And our journeys today are much the same.
Whether you're a shepherd or a king
A doctor, a dustman, or any other thing
From different places our God is able,
To guide our paths to the King in the stable!

I had been in a different place that year, walking through a personal breakdown and professional failure. My return to this story was not insignificant and in that retelling of the story in a way children would understand I had a return, in a unique way, to myself. I saw the King in the stable in a new, more authentic way. As I reconciled myself to the broken journey that I had completed over the previous six months, I began to see it as an opportunity for creativity to live. Participation in something millennia-old does that for your soul. Let us paint, draw, sew and sing this story with our children. It is probable then that they might see that this story is not only yours, but in a real and tangible way, it is also theirs, and perhaps most importantly, it is theirs to share.

Christmas Films

No more let sin or sorrow grow,
Nor thorns infest the ground!
He comes to make his blessings known,
Far as the curse is found.

This little book is too short to debate the complex and ongoing arguments concerning the status of 'Die Hard' as a Christmas movie. It comes around each year and will continue forever, there are advocates on both sides and by not taking a position, I have offended everyone, fantastic.

However, I am going to take a strong position about another action film. In my mind, there is no debate, the ultimate and most profound Christmas film is in fact 'Children of Men.' It was released on Christmas Day 2006 in the United States to critical and public acclaim. It is based on the novel by P.D James and stars Clive Owen. I rarely enjoy a book to film adaptation. In this case, the book is a study in aging and living with hopelessness and the film is an action-packed thriller that stabs at the heart of our sense of self-sufficiency.

The story is a dystopian one in which there have been no pregnancies in the entire world for over eighteen years. Schools lay empty, the world is dying, and Britain is the only country continuing in any kind of civilised fashion. There is a growing problem on the borders as refugees from less stable countries threaten Britain's perceived security.

Britain is aging and the sense of hopelessness and the sounds of weeping are prevalent throughout the film. Various groups or cults arise to suggest extreme behaviours to combat the situation, they are short-lived and replaced quickly by another more extreme group. Cages of refugees are visible on the streets of London and Britain's are unable to escape from the reality they face.

Owen's character, Theo, is a civil servant. His job is to serve and protect the British people. He is a classic civil servant, although way too handsome for the job. Even his cheerful optimism and stiff upper lip are starting to crack. There is a rumour growing in London about a *fugee* girl being pregnant and a group called the Tomorrow People who want to get her to safety. Theo gets caught up in this rumour and discovers it is true. There is a black, single, refugee female who is nearly 9 months pregnant. Owen's demeanour when he sees her body swollen with hope brings tears to my eyes even as I type today. There is a brief joke where she claims to be a virgin and then this monologue that describes the life growing inside her belly, it is one of the most powerful sequences in cinema. Che, pronounced Key, must be moved to safety as the pressure on this young woman and her child is unbelievable. There is an incredible action sequence that lasts about forty-five minutes, and the novel gives about 3 sentences, but that's another story. Theo and Che with the help of several others arrive at a camp where supposedly there will be a ship later. At the most inconvenient time, Che starts to go into labour and her waters break as the bombs and gunfire begin to fill the air.

Che labours in a bombed-out block of flats, in a refugee camp that used to be Bexhill on Sea. Bombs and war going on around her. The cinematographer makes it clear that at this point society has disintegrated so much that no one is sure, least of all the audience, what they are fighting toward, their goal is unclear. They are destroying each other as their hope for the future has unravelled.

Theo, Owen's character, provides rudimentary midwifery services, and hopeless attempts to remind Che to breathe and push. The flat is bombed out so as a male he cannot even be sent for ice chips. His ineptitude and hopelessness juxtaposed to the birth of hope and the exhausted determination of a passionate mother. Finally, silence. Broken by that fragile, vulnerable unmistakable cry of new birth.

A GIRL.

Theo and Che leave the bombed-out flat with the new child and as they walk through the centre of the warzone the baby cries and the gunfire ceases. There is a holy silence, as soldiers, who seconds before, were bent on killing each other, weep, as the child passes through their midst. They remove their helmets, and some walk away from their feud as hope for the first time in two decades walks in their midst. I will not spoil the end of the film for you, but I will say this truth; the best films are the ones that ask questions. This film asks two profound questions:

1. Why are you weeping?
2. Why do you hope?

The world is falling apart and cannot save itself, infertility has impacted everyone, rich and poor and in between. Civilisation is effectively ending. I hope because there is an unlikely girl who carries hope in her fragile broken body. The most vulnerable form of hope lives inside the woman. The message of Christmas is clear as day.

At the other end of the scale entirely, in terms of films at least, there is a sign of Christmas that appears each year, the feel-good Christmas movie. On the Hallmark channel, they have one for every day in December. They seem to follow a formulaic plotline. Woman with a tragic backstory, in distress either personally, professionally, or both. There is often an additional challenge that must be solved by December 25th that makes the situation appear as if it is falling apart. Cue the arrival of a handsome, but mysterious man. Sidenote, these men often bear a striking resemblance to another, far more famous actor, I usually spend most of the film trying to put their face to a different name. As the plotline continues a twist appears that seems to indicate final devastation. Then, just in time for Christmas Eve, the miscommunication is clarified; disaster is averted and a new, more beautiful, balance is restored to the universe. Typically, the man and woman fall into a saccharin ridden type of love and live happily ever after.

These films ask the same profound questions as 'Children of Men' and provide the same answers. My world is falling apart, and a man is bringing hope.

As a feminist, I hate that these films exist, as a follower of Jesus I see them as a sign of Christmas and greater than that as a sign of the story of Christmas that asks the question, why are you weeping? Humanity is walking in darkness, hurting each other, caught up in a web of behaviours that hurt and destroy each other. Why do I hope? Because an unlikely girl in a far-off land has hope within her body and that hope is the hope for all humanity.

Asking these questions and one more significant question is another Christmas film, 'It's A Wonderful Life.' Has my life mattered? The main character George Bailey finds himself at a crisis point on one Christmas Eve when he finds himself wondering if he has made an impact on the community he has invested into his entire life. From the outside, it appears that he has been living a life where his dreams have not come true. He has been prevented from his dreams by outside forces and circumstances that derail him just before he breaks free several times through the film. I just want to add that this film asks another invaluable question, one that hits hard at the centre of the human psyche. Has my life mattered? We are humans wired for connection, wired for community. We also know that we want to have influence. George Bailey goes on a long journey through time to discover that his influence was deep. It was limited to one small town, but he went a long way with them. His history was intertwined and the people he rescued went a long way. Many of them went further than him and would not have had the opportunity without his sacrifice. It is not that way for everyone. Some people have a wide influence, a shallow pool with a large group of people. We can all make a difference. We answer the question. Like I said earlier, the best films ask questions. The best stories ask questions and expect us to find an answer within ourselves. George asks this question: Has my life mattered? He has lived a sacrificial life and discovers that he has friends and relationships within which he has mattered. Is that the influence and success he thought he wanted? No, probably not. There are so many people who are searching for influence in the wrong place that asking the question, how do I want my life to matter? will unlock some fantastic conversations with people, young and old.

So, if you err on the side of Die Hard being a Christmas movie, watch it with some friends. Whether you do or not, you can watch a true Christmas film 'Children of Men' and ask your friends why they are weeping and why do they hope? For those of you who love a good Hallmark film fest, watch your Hallmark Christmas films this year and ask the questions of your friends and neighbours that these films do, you will be surprised by their answers. Whatever you do this Christmas season remember the famous line to George Bailey at the end of 'It's A Wonderful Life.' No man is a failure who has friends.

Cards and Greetings

Have yourself a merry little Christmas
Let your heart be light
From now on your troubles will be out of sight
Have yourself a merry little Christmas
Make the Yuletide gay
From now on your troubles will be miles away
Here we are as in olden days
Happy golden days of yore
Faithful friends who are dear to us
Gather near to us once more
Through the years we all will be together
If the fates allow
Hang a shining star upon the highest place
So have yourself a merry little Christmas
Have yourself a merry little Christmas
So have yourself a merry little Christmas

'Why did you say that?' I looked confused at the woman in front of me. A friend, I had known for a long time. She continued:

'It's Merry Christmas and Happy New Year.'

It took my mind a few moments to compute where her head was in this space. In her head, there was a correct way to say the festive greeting and 'Happy Christmas,' a phrase common in my native England, was incorrect. I shrugged and said I had no idea, it was just the way it was, and if I am honest, it did not seem that important to me. The heart behind the greeting was more important, surely? I could not be more wrong. As the culture war intensified, the battle for the phrase 'Merry Christmas' intensified as well. I am an introvert and do not care much for talking to anyone in public. My extroverted friends love to shout and cheer to strangers and new phrases entered their post-thanksgiving vernacular. Phrases like 'Seasons Greetings' or 'Happy Holidays.' American friends of mine who worked retail were instructed to use these phrases exclusively. People had been offended by 'Merry Christmas' and apparently had complained. I have a hard time believing this, with a strong undercurrent of life being too short, right? But I have never swallowed a button and the average person swallows three buttons in their lifetime.

For a few years, I went along with them and the desire to not cause offence. It felt hospitable to say, 'Seasons Greetings' as opposed to 'Merry Christmas.' I wanted to welcome everyone, but the phrase felt hollow. The war intensified, outrage, followed by inaction, over red cups, and I wanted all the noise to stop.

Part of me considered the phrase 'If you can't say anything nice, don't say anything at all.' It had a part to play in this conversation, but nice is such a non-word, it is synthetic. Perhaps I wish the phrase was 'if you can't say anything meaningful, shut up!' Yes, it might be brutal, but that is my desire. I think that is why instead of saying Happy Holidays, I started going quiet.

A chill sneer not of derision, well, maybe derision but not for the phrase itself but for the lack of sincerity and depth it contained.

Times changed, the debate continued, and I returned to the United Kingdom. On the whole, a Christmas obsessed nation. It starts somewhere in early September, but the greetings fly from mid-November. Britain is diverse, people of all faiths and none make their home in our melting pot, but the wishing of 'Happy Christmas' is ubiquitous. No one seems offended. I asked my Facebook friends what they look forward to as a sign of Christmas and one of my friends who is atheist said 'wishing people a Happy Christmas.' The greeting is cheery in our northern climes, where the daylight is short, to hear something, it starts the anticipation. Is this part of the sacred nature of Advent? That those who may not believe whisper to weary saints of His coming. What a delightful thought.
My most sacred interaction with this notion came in 2017. I was working as a tutor. Freelance work, it was low stress, low preparation, and some of the most delight-filled work I have completed on this earth.

I worked for a large extended Muslim family who lived in close proximity to one another. Two sets of cousins are all girls, and during the year I got to know all of them quite well. One of the daughters confided that I was the only non-Muslim person who had ever been in their home. There was press coverage during that time of the behaviour of ISIS and all the attacks. It was a privilege to sit with these peace-loving families and reassure them of their welcome and my appreciation of their culture and community. It was getting closer to Christmas, and I think it was my last tutoring session before the Christmas break. I was bundling up and getting ready to leave and awkwardly waiting for the money. The Father of the house came down the stairs slowly. He thrust the cash into my hand, and I turned to leave. He was an older man, an Imam at the local mosque, passionate about his faith and committed to passing the tradition on to his children. He was equally passionate about preparing his children for a better life than he led. He goes to open the door for me and as he opens the door says:

'Serena, are you a follower, are you a Christian?'

My heart bounces to my mouth for a second. It has not ended well for Christians who have answered this question affirmatively when asked by Muslims recently. I remember his gentle brown eyes and the trust he puts in me as an educator of his children. I remember his head shaking and the brief conversation we had surrounding the draconian immigration policies. I blush, embarrassed, not at the question, but my moment of fear. I have unconscious bias and I have just reckoned with it.

'Yes, Ajaz.'

I respond, it comes out quiet, a holy moment.
He sighs gently.

'Well then, have a holy, sacred and most satisfying Christmas.'

He pauses, and then with a smile adds:

'Happy Christmas.'

The phrase 'thank you' seems such an inadequate response to the sacred silence between me and this expressive greeting. Their acknowledgement that this time of year has a holy significance for me, his generosity in tone and thought. A moment I almost missed due to fear and bias. I sat in the car for a moment and marvelled at this man of peace and his statement. Our ideologies differ, our expression of faith looks different, but to honour my hope for the festival of my faith as holy and sacred affirmed my position that perhaps if you cannot say anything meaningful, shutting up is the best way to communicate. My friends who say 'Happy Holidays' miss these moments of generosity. The hospitable moments when our sacred hope finds expression in unlikely places. Perhaps, if we could all see the sacred image of God in every human, we would get closer to peace on earth. After all, it starts with goodwill toward men.

In his book Christmas: Its Origins and Associations William Dawson says this:

'I have observed that whatever view men hold respecting Christ they all agree that His Advent is to be hailed with joy, and the nearer the forms of festivity have approximated to the teaching of Him who is being celebrated the more real has been the joy of those who have taken part in the celebrations.'

This research seems to back up my point that silence is the best antidote to superficiality. This position is probably why I am terrible at sending Christmas Cards promptly. I have the best of intentions. I purchase boxes of them regularly and announce to friends and family, and anyone else who will listen, this year is the year I send Christmas cards. Then, I write two or three each year. I get carried away writing epistles the length of 'War and Peace' full of words of affirmation and appreciation for the recipient, I do not see the point of writing 'To Such a body and so and so from Serena' on three hundred cards. I want to say what I have admired and appreciated over the past year. I want to call to life within them, something that may have been dormant in their personality. I want the card to mean something. Do you think my love language might be words of affirmation?

The paradox that we can sometimes find ourselves caught inside is that we receive a card from somebody, and it reminds us of their existence. The impact they have had on our lives and the memories of times we have shared flood our bodies. Sometimes though, it causes shame, perhaps guilt, or recalls a negative experience, we have tried to forget. The inevitable presence of a round-robin newsletter pulls us into a tailspin of comparison where we often end up at the bottom of the pile. Even if we do not have a ten-year-old who came 5th in the annual conker championship at the parish fair, we feel like we should have one, and damn it, coach them to at least make the podium. I have friends who send a newsletter each year, with a quiz for the readers to participate in, in their Christmas card. I met up with their adult children and commented that I had won the quiz in our family in the most recent year. She said her goal is to do nothing noteworthy during 2020 in hopes of having nothing to say in the newsletter. Her goal was pretty much answered but not quite in the way she had expected! Is there a way to stand back from this whirlwind of comparison, celebrate the good and acknowledge the adversities with authenticity? Is there?

Perhaps there is, perhaps the answer is to move away from the minutiae of daily life to more universal and existential visions of life. In the 1800s, as the industrial revolution provided more disposable income for people, and separated them from immediate and extended families, Christmas cards rapidly increased in their popularity. These original cards contained short prayers or poems rich with meaning and affection. Here is an example by Edwin Markham a popular author of the day:

My thoughts go out to you my friend,
This Happy Christmas time,
Wishing you joy in all your deeds and days.
Wishing you time for the task,
Wisdom for the work,
Peace for the pathway
Friends for the fireside
And love to the last.

I think that is wonderful. They are the exact elements I pray for all my friends often, joy, time, wisdom, peace, and love. Saturated with meaning without being the length of Swann's Way.

I need to add that this does not mean the Victorians had it all sorted when it came to Christmas greetings and traditions. One of the earliest Christmas cards I found during my research was a picture of a dead robin, lying on his back in the snow. Underneath, it said 'Have a Jolly Christmas.' One must wonder if there was any communication between the designer and the copywriter. Better yet if whoever was proofreading their Christmas Cards had any training in sensitivity and tone. Also, who would buy such a thing, and send it? Well, the one I found was sent from Charles to Mary. Perhaps the message inside read 'you have survived this year, the robin did not, have a jolly Christmas.'

This brings me back to the earlier poem by Edwin Markham with its authentic and yet still generic greeting for his friends. It seems in the mass production of Christmas we have lost some of that authenticity. One of my oldest friends draws a handmade card each year. She has the image reproduced hundreds of times. Inside is a specific message for that year that she has prayed about and thought through. I look forward to receiving her card each year. Maybe I will do that this year, she said for the twentieth year in a row, or maybe, like Ajaz, my Islamic friend, I will pray, and send a card to each of you requesting that you have a holy, sacred, and satisfying festival. – Selah

Food and Feasting

Chestnuts roasting on an open fire,
Jack Frost nipping at your nose,
Though it's been said many times, many ways
Merry Christmas to you!

Lockdown three in the United Kingdom, which started at the tail end of December 2020, was the toughest for me. I lost three friends and extended family members in the first weeks of January and by the end of the month, I was depleted, emotionally and physically. The days just seemed so monotonous, and the weather was cold and dark. Some friends and I booked onto a virtual chocolate making class so that we would have something to focus our days towards. Something that inspired us to keep going. Chocolate has a way of achieving that exact thing.

At the end of a sticky afternoon at the beginning of March, I was left with many imperfectly formed, totally delicious chocolate truffles. More than I should eat myself. I mean, I could eat them, no doubt of that, but 'should,' it is different than could. I shared some with a friend, outside and socially distanced. Feeling a need for full disclosure, this friend, was my personal trainer, which says something of my lack of commitment to the fitness process. I mean, I went to a chocolate making class and not only told him about it; I also gave him some of the treats. His comment struck me, in both the profundity and simplicity of his response:

'I enjoyed the chocolates you made, they reminded me of something my aunty makes at Christmas.'

It was my first attempt at chocolate making and I transported someone, in the height of lockdown isolation, to a moment of family and community. An altogether happier time. Even if I did want to smash his face in moments later, as the kettlebell, once again proved, that gravity exists.

Food is evocative. Christmas food is more than anything else. It has the power to transport us. Ask a group of people the one thing that makes Christmas dinner and they would probably each give you a different answer. Ask each of those people to bring their favourite, or most traditional Christmas food, to your house for dinner and you would feast on more than food. Memories, stories, and connections would be present in your home but more of that later.

One of the signs that Christmas is coming is the special food that appears in our stores each year. It bothers me that it appears each year earlier and earlier. I ate a mince pie at the end of August last year; its sell-by date was November third. Before Advent calendars were filled with chocolate or gin, Advent was a time of solemn fasting, it functioned in a similar way to the lent season. To remind ourselves of the yearning and the patient waiting of our ancestors who died waiting for the promise to be fulfilled. Then on the Twenty Fourth of December, commenced twelve days of full out feasting and celebration. If we look back into history, we can see the menus were vast, elaborate affairs and the feasting and celebration went on for days. King John's feast in 1213 consisted of 24 hogshead of wine, 200 heads of pork, 1,000 hens. If that was not enough and perhaps for the pescatarians among us he also ordered 10,000 salt eels. Suddenly, it makes our turkey dinner and bubble, and squeak leftovers seem a little less extravagant.

I wonder if we dialled back our Christmas feasting to begin on December 24th if we would be good and hungry in a different way. Our souls may be slightly more engaged with the process and our minds would be freer to enjoy the celebration without the anxiety of weight gain. 2020 was an anomaly but often by Christmas Eve, I've eaten about five Christmas dinners, and I am ready for something different. Sneaking a lockdown visit to my family, my mum announced that she'd made beef wellington. I almost left and went somewhere else. I am all about the late December cheese coma, but sometimes by the time the day arrives, much like the very hungry caterpillar, I want some leaves, a glass of soda water, and a day of fasting.

Our medieval ancestors seemed to see this connection, more clearly than we do, in both directions. As well as an elaborate feast for the nobles and their families there is overwhelming evidence that, at the darkest hour of the year, when the poorest were at a distinct disadvantage. Survival, through the winter months, may not have been inevitable. The rich and noble in each area would distribute large parcels of food for the poor to enable them to survive the winter. In his book, Christmas: Its Origins and Associations, William Dawson says this:

There was an outflow of generous hospitality to the poor, who had a hard time of it during the rest of the year, and who required the Christmas gifts to provide them with such creature comforts as would help them through the inclement season of the year.

It seems it was much more than money thrown in a bucket, but a connection, the kind only forged by shared experience and humanity. Gifts have a way of making people feel seen.

There was a Welsh Baron in the Middle Ages who took this idea of hospitality and shared experience a little further during the Christmas period. He held a huge feast, where everyone was invited. To express how serious he was, when he said everyone was invited, if you turned up, you came in and feasted at the table. No one was allowed to ask about your identity for at least three days. By then, of course, most people were too drunk or too well acquainted to remove someone who was considered an interloper.

I love this idea! Our Christmas gatherings would be fascinating if we had a truly open home and whoever arrived would be made welcome and fed well. They may find themselves in a community for the first time, and one day you may find a welcome where you least expected it.

For several years I lived in the States and travelling at Christmas was expensive and often traumatic. I could write a book about my experience trying to get home for Christmas during the great freeze of 2010. Which consisted of about 5 and a half inches of snow in London. After my four-day journey, there was nothing I wanted more than my Mum's leeks in the cheese sauce and my dad's take on the gin and tonic. It was a Gin with a hint of tonic, but after four days and nights in various airports that was the necessary treatment for my trauma.

However, the sting and sometimes impossibility of travel have yielded the fruit of a wide view of the nature and constituent parts of the Christmas Feast. There is plenty of room for the beige foods that we seem to consume with joy in December, but I have added Jack Daniel's Chocolate Pecan Pie to my Christmas Feasting requirements and my life is richer for the experience. It also means there is a different choice than Christmas pudding available which means no one must pretend they enjoy it. I introduced American friends to

Parmesan Crusted Roast Parsnip Now they prepare them religiously each year. As part of the feast, Christmas Crackers are now firmly a part of the Christmas tradition in several homes I shared the day with over the years. I am transported to Christmases in Saint Louis by Chocolate Peanut butter fudge and crab cakes. Both homemade, delicious, and not something my family would have known about without my United States family and relationships. Our experiences of shared foods have made our lives richer and more interconnected. Every dish has a story. If we could find a way to open our homes, like the Welsh Baron without questioning someone's right to be there, we could find our lives enriched by food and friends that transport us to their homes even though they are far away. Food with a story is my invitation each year with a group of friends. Early in December I host a potluck/ bring and share a meal with friends who span ages, nations, and world views. Each guest is invited to bring a dish to share, the caveat is that each person must tell the story of the dish and share the recipe for each person to take home. It really is a fantastic evening. Relationships deepen, tears and laughter are shared, as we feast. People remember the food as well; our lives are interconnected as we eat together.

Earlier, I said that Advent was a time of fasting and I've just written about a feast in early December. I think my heart is that our Christmas feasts would reflect more closely the tone of everyone is welcome and valued and has something to bring, rather than our picture-perfect meals where everyone and every meal looks the same. Would it take a massive shift to include someone who looked, or perhaps more dangerously thought differently to us? Maybe the first year, but after a shared experience, we often find ourselves craving those different dishes that have evoked a sense of interconnected community, for the first time. After all, connection not perfection is where true joy exists. The feast is about creating and holding a place where everyone has a voice at the table. Everyone, a story to share about how they have survived, and a contribution that will connect us to their story and our shared history.

Decorations

Deck the Halls with boughs of Holly,
Fa, la, la, la, la, la, la, la, la.
'Tis the season to be jolly
Fa, la, la, la, la, la, la, la, la.

I was a theatre major in college. I studied English as well, but the theatre was where my heart got excited. One of my favourite classes, which shaped me as a young director, was semiotics. The philosophy and language of signs. What do they mean, and more importantly, how do we use them? We studied images for hours and debated their meaning into the night. It has caused me no end of joy in adult life to be able to pick apart a movie or something and decipher the message. Sadly, it destroyed several M. Night Shamylan films as I figured out the twists within the first ten minutes.

A quick lesson in signs before we start talking about decorations as a sign or symbol of Christmas. Icons are the simplest to understand. They are a direct representation of what they represent. All tv shows and films are iconic. It is a direct representation of the story they are trying to tell. It is not happening, but the actors are accurately representing their characters. The red traffic light person and the schematised figure on the door of the toilet. They are simple signs that have a direct relationship to the thing they represent and are universally understood.

Index signs only take on meaning when you see them in a relationship with something else. You ask me where the donkey is, and I point with my *index* finger. You know the location of the donkey. An arrow has no meaning until you attach the phrase Accident and Emergency beforehand. Suddenly, you know where to go when you are bleeding from the jugular. These kinds of signs are very useful if you are lost and are trying to find your way. At least they were before Google

Symbolic signs have no direct relationship to their signifiers. Instead, they require an agreement from a group of people who subscribe to the convention of their meaning. For example, we have all agreed that the letters C.A.T spell cat. We have all agreed that the red circle with the white line through the middle means no entry and that the 15-foot inflatable penguin is the perfect sign that Christmas is coming. We can similarly deduce, that the house behind it is full of Christmas cheer. As I began thinking about this as a concept, I became more than a little confused and wanted to go back to the beginning. I wanted to discover how we got to this point. As from my cursory knowledge of the nativity story, along with the lobster, penguins were not present at the birth of Christ! My research took me to an interesting place, so join me as we look together at decorations as a sign of Christmas.

Francis of Assisi could not talk to animals. There, I said it. He did, however, talk to the animals to make a statement against the wealthy in his community. He implied that they were so unresponsive to his message of simple living that he may as well have talked to the animals. He did in fact, preach a sermon to the birds, as the world's first object lesson. This event started the legend that he could talk to animals. This book is not a revisionist history of the life of Francis of Assisi; although, I love to burst bubbles of innocence! He is here because he is attributed with starting one of the signs of Christmas. The Christmas decoration. It seems that this effort filled accoutrements, like many of the other traditions we have examined, started simply. It seems they started as a trio of hand-carved wooden animals. A simple nativity scene of a cow, a donkey, and a sheep gathered around an empty manger. This fact makes me wonder what he would say, if, in some, Bill and Ted Esque adventure we brought this saint to our modern-day homes adorned with giant snowmen, flying reindeer, and woolly hat endorsed penguins. My guess is we would find a confused saint talking to the inflatable reindeer proclaiming a message of sacred simplicity.

If we think about our modern celebrations, it does seem that we may have lost our way a little. I do love to look at decorations. They light up our northern darkness and are so very cheerful on a gloomy December evening. The message they send is somewhat synthetic. A flying reindeer or a ten-foot penguin wearing a hat offers the viewer a moment of comfort or a quick smile, nothing more. These enormous creatures wobble from side to side bedecked in a scarf and bobble hat. Am I the only person who wonders how they adorn themselves with these items given their lack of hands and elbows?

The generosity of the act ends in the middle of January when the credit card bills hit, and the decorations lay flat on the grass. Signs and symbols, which I believe decorations are, point us to something deeper. If we look at the penguin as a metaphor, I think it is perfect. It is almost sinister the fake thing points to a reality that when the money runs out, we are deflated and lay distorted and disorientated on the ground. Decorations are a symbol, and they point to something else. They are an external picture of what is our internal reality. Culture is religion externalised. These images of penguins dancing in the winter are a picture of what we worship. The visual and aural signs that we share betray our society's beliefs about itself. These inflatable penguins point to a dancing singing reality that is sustained until Blue Monday.

The third Monday in January, which is considered to be the saddest day of the year as the credit card bills hit, the days are still short, the festive season is over. On top of that, there are more suicides that day than any other in the year. Then we spend the rest of the year trying to pay off the bills to create the fake reality again the following year.

Is the solution an inflatable nativity scene that sways to the tune of 'Oh Little Town of Bethlehem?' I am not convinced that is the answer. Those lighted nativity scenes are a little bit creepy, and the people are far too white and clean to be an accurate representation of the birth of Christ.

The answer is not an austere, dutiful, almost puritan return stripped back to essentials and nothing ostentatious. For, we will die if we allow our symbols of love to be defined by our duty rather than our soaring vision. The truth is that decorations are much like the index symbols I wrote about earlier. They find their meaning when attached to a relationship with a person. They are an outward symbol of the impact the birth of Christ has meant for your life. Decorations may be symbols that ask questions. Questions that can only be answered through the context of a relationship. I have one such decoration in my limited collection. It is a glass ornament, a suncatcher, in the shape, colour and texture of a sunrise. I received it   from one of my friends with the gift buying gene. It has nothing to do with the Christmas story; except that it asks the question: why is that a Christmas decoration? I will only share that story in the context of a relationship, so hit me up for a coffee and I will tell you all about the story. For those of you, who think that you know the ornament's connection to the Christmas story, I am confident you will be surprised by the answer.

So, put up your decorations this year, look at your collection of ornaments, remember the stories and memories that you associate with them. Tell those stories and perhaps add a few that confuse or intrigue your friends. These may lead to some great conversations and point to a reality more true, more authentic, and more real than the inflatable penguins could ever hope to illustrate. Of course, this reality is only accessed through the context of a relationship.

Silence

How Silently, how silently,
The wondrous gift is given.
So, God imparts to human hearts
The message of his heaven.

There is always a moment, after the last present has been opened, or when we finally push the plate away with full stomachs. Maybe it is the moment when someone passes on a purple quality street. A pause, a moment of appreciative awe. A moment when we finally reach the point where we say enough is enough. A satisfied sigh emits from our soul. A moment of pure contentment. Peaceful joy. A moment to take stock, and realise all that we possess, also possesses us to a certain extent. That moment of restful, contented silence could be the highlight of the year.

Silence is powerful. It is charged with emotion. Silence seems to communicate, even to the most unaware of us, that a situation is at hand. If you have ever walked into a room, where two people have just stopped arguing, you will understand what I mean by silence communicates. The phrase silence is deafening is accurate.

It is true at the opposite end of the scale as well. At the end of a magnificent concert or other thrilling live performance, there is always a moment. A silence filled with ecstasy. A moment where time seems to stand still and hang in the air, like Michael Jordan, and then it is disrupted by applause.

December is noisy! From beginning to end it grabs at our attention and focus. Parties, music, crowds, and bustle. Even my extroverted friends find themselves ready for a quiet week or two at the beginning of January. Ask my friends, with January birthdays about the struggle with trying to organise their birthday celebrations.

It is as if the world were full, and may I suggest overloaded? Similar to the way, after a large meal, we need a moment to let all that we have experienced and tasted die down. For the last few years, I have done that exact thing at the beginning of January. I take a day to be silent and reflect on the previous year to look at my life and consider the highs, lows, and growth. Have I grown in peace? Is there more or less self-control in my life? Have I experienced, and exhibited joy at times when the circumstances would have dictated otherwise? I am honest, to the extreme, in my reflections. From those moments I make my goals for the year. Not on New Year's Day, as a reaction, to a few too many drinks at the late-night celebrations, the previous evening. Instead, I move from a place of silence, a place of peace. Even at the most troubling moments, this practice has calmed the hurricane within and outside my soul.

The eye of the hurricane is the quietest place to exist. The storm rages around you: a silent centre is a safe place. Could it be that those rare moments of silence that are full of wonder and contentment are available to us all the time? We live our lives in such a hurry especially in the frenetic build-up to Christmas. That when the moment of contentment arrives, we are uncomfortable with it and rush to the next moment before we have given it time to impact our souls. The challenge, on the flip side of that discomfort, is that we seem to wait for Christmas to exhaust us before we can reach that point of contentment. Researchers tell us, and anecdotal experience backs up the idea, that our creativity, ingenuity, and especially our capacity are increased when we start from a place of rest, not pressure. We know that when we set the pace for our lives, in accordance with our level of peace, we are more content. Yet we allow other expectations, that many of us have, to crash in so regularly, that we are constantly harried. We wait for silence to come to us, and yet quiet, peace and silence are ours to create. I write this as a single person who lives alone and often finds that silence is available. It is easier for me than many others. It is simply a case of putting the mobile phone down and sitting for a minute. For those with more limits on their time, let me suggest a five-minute sit in the car or house, every day, after the school run, during December. Five minutes of contentment to push away the plate, to marvel at all that we have and allow our Advent preparations to begin from a place of contentment and peace, rather than frantic, hurried, exhaustion. I have a friend with several young children who starts each day, after the school run, with a five-minute sit in silence in her minivan.

I am not suggesting that we become monks hating our lives and rejecting all possessions, but the opposite. Let us become a deeply connected and committed community that do not let external circumstances dictate our activity. Instead, from a place of silence, serve, love, and welcome others in true hospitality aware that silence is a sign of the contentment available to us, all day, every day.

Father Christmas

So, I will dance with Cinderella
While she is here in my arms
'Cause I know something the prince never knew
Oh, I will dance with Cinderella
I don't wanna miss even one song
'Cause all too soon the clock will strike midnight
And she'll be gone

Something comes alive in me when I am near water. I love being by the seaside. I love the rhythm of the waves. I love the sting of saltwater on sunburned skin. The way the sun seems to hang on the horizon and then suddenly disappear. I discover a sense of childlike glee and abandon when I first see the ocean, or the lake, or even a canal.

I love to sit and watch the water and, to be honest, I like to feel small. It seems to happen to me in a unique way when I sit and watch the water. It is a holiday tradition of mine to sit by the sea, until I realise just how small I am, in comparison to the magnificent ocean. This Summer I was away with some friends searching for just that experience. The weight of the world and its turmoil were on my shoulders. I wanted to feel small. I was walking by myself, by the water, when I discovered an abandoned sandcastle fort. Someone had built a collection of small sandcastles, in a near-perfect square, with a bigger fort in the middle. Lunch or something had called them away and it was deserted.

A few minutes later, my friends caught up with me. They are fairly serious people. We sat there, the three of us for about twenty minutes and pelted rocks at the sandcastles from about fifteen feet away. We made up stories about the imaginary town we were destroying. The town had long been abandoned. No-one was injured and a new eco village with zero emissions. A new and just utopia was going to be built in its place We cheered when someone had a particularly good hit on a castle.

In the interest of full disclosure, we missed more than we hit and none of us is a particularly good aim. There was no point in our activity and there were no regulations on how the activity was conducted. It was pure, childlike play. That evening at a rather nice supper, to celebrate the last night of our holiday the discussion turned to that moment. We all agreed that it was a highlight of the holiday. We are all adults with serious jobs. Them, more than me, as I struggle to take anything too seriously, talking about throwing rocks at a sandcastle as a highlight of our time together. Later that evening we found and attended a free firework display that was also a moment of pure delight. Both activities had no point to them, they were just ours to enjoy. In both these activities, we were playful.

What has this got to do with the mythical creature that dominates the Christmas season and brings presents to small children? Well, it is so fun to pretend. It is so very fun to play. To enter an imaginary journey with the children in your life. There is a place for adulthood and honesty and growing up comes with responsibility. There is also a place to put off those things and to enter an idea that something impossible could take place. Magic can happen and joy can be manifest.

The origins of Father Christmas are well known. He is a real historical figure. Saint Nicholas was born circa 280 in Patara, Lycia, an area that is part of present-day Turkey. He lost both of his parents as a young man and reportedly used his inheritance to help the poor and sick. A devout Christian, he later served as bishop of Myra, a city that is now called Demre. His charity and generosity developed into a mythical benevolent timeless creature. You know the story; he flies all over the world in one evening and delivers gifts to good children. Any quick google search could tell you his origin story. You know that children queue to see him, you know that the bubble bursts for each child. I also know that people have incredibly strong opinions on whether inviting your children into this story is good parenting. I do not want to, nor can I with any integrity write about this issue. There is only one thing I want to say about Father Christmas, and it comes back to the rocks on the beach, fireworks, and the suspension of disbelief.

This little book is fraught with meaning. Its unpublished subtitle is Signs of Christmas: meaning in the mayhem. Throughout, I have tried to explore some of our behaviours, and explore the nuance and delight of their meaning for us in the twenty-first century. I have looked at signs and symbols and all other things. When it comes to Father Christmas, what I want to say most of all is that its point is to be entirely pointless. It is entirely without meaning, and that is its primary purpose. It is fun to pretend. To play a game with children and invite them in their innocence to believe in something entirely meaningless. It is good for us as adults to participate in these kinds of activities. It is good for us, deep in our souls, to put off the armour of adulthood and to play. There is merit for our souls in participating in this game. Admitting that we love to pretend, and we need to play. We need to throw more rocks at sandcastles, gaze at the lingering fireworks and believe for one or two minutes every December that this fun game could be true.

So, dress up, like Father Christmas or an elf. Ask a child what they hope Father Christmas will bring them in their stocking. Suspend belief about gravity, speed, and time, for an instant. Being an adult has so many responsibilities, we face so many difficult decisions and heart troubling moments. So, stop for a moment and play. The world needs more play, more laughter and more reckless abandon.

So?

The fire is dying
Now my lamp is growing dim
The shades of night are lifting
The morning light steals across my windowpane
Where webs of snow are drifting

If I could only, have you near
To breathe a sigh or two
I would be happy just to hold the hands I love
On this winter night with you
And to be once again with you

When I was a teacher of English, my young students had the privilege of working through 'How to Read a Book' by the legend that is Mortimer Adler. He had four questions one should ask when reading a book, and the last of them was 'And what of it?' I was trying to be the 'trendy, hip and down with the kids' teacher', so I allowed them to refer to the last question as 'So?'

And that is my question and the end of this little book that has explored some of the signs that Christmas is coming. I cannot go back to the exhausted, perfectionistic celebrations of Christmas that have left me feeling dog tired and fed up with people by December 20th.

The guiding principles for me moving forward in my authentic expression of Christmas:

Community over the Individual: I am convinced that, in this digital age, we need real relationships, with real people, more than ever. I am also convinced that we need to put ourselves around people who will tell us the story of their Christmas from a different perspective. We have been able to manipulate our environments to suit us to the tiniest detail and moment of our lives. However, it is not good for us to be in that kind of control. You only have to watch the frustration when we cannot control something insignificant to know that we were designed to be more accustomed to discomfort. In this season of goodwill and peace to all men I want to be the kind of person, like my Muslim friend Ajaz who honours the sacred in other people's stories. I want to sit and listen to the story of the pork pie that your grandpa made each year that will always remind you of childhood joy. I want to laugh at the jokes and the quirky traditions like the lucky carrot in the gravy. They may not be mine, but if you tell the story well enough, I will see that this narrative is a part of what makes me human. It will be especially potent if my Christmas stories become a part of your tradition and together, we build a rich tapestry from every nation under heaven committed to sharing life and showing love to everyone. This Christmas I will choose meals, moments and memories that promote the community over the individual. It is not acceptable that many people express that Christmas is the hardest time of the year. Is there a spare seat at your table? That is the wrong question. Do you have more than you need? (Hint: The answer is yes) then build a bigger table and invite someone to share their story. You will all be better off for the experience.

Meaning over Niceties: This season I will write Christmas cards full of encouragement to friends who have walked with me over this year. I will end them with a heartfelt closing unique to that person that fills their heart with wisdom. I will wish every shop worker a Merry Christmas from the end of Thanksgiving until the 6th of January. I will purchase a few gifts that have value and contain meaning for the people that will receive them. I will choose the holy sacred, even if my voice shakes as I speak. I will choose some meaningful decorations, adorn my real tree with apples. Invite friends to a feast and insist that they tell a story or two of their Christmas traditions and memories. I may even burn my tree on Christmas Eve and toast a marshmallow or two on its flames.

Showing over telling: This may seem like a bit of a contradiction in terms seeing as I have just spent almost 30,000 words telling you my thoughts about our Christmas traditions. However, showing people the way of peace amidst turmoil is absolutely the conclusion at which I have arrived. Be that advent calendar chocolate that your friends and family need. Find a way to make those around you hungry for the good stuff that is coming, even if we don't see it at all yet. Define the moment that anchors their soul in hope and raises their peace amid anxiety. I will play along and indulge the childhood fantasies of the children in my life, because it is good for me to play. It is good for us all if we play more.

Finally, I will use words full of meaning to close and wish you all a holy, sacred, and satisfying festival. – Selah.

Bibliography

Pg. 7 Lightfoot, G. (1967). Song for a Winter's Night. New York, New York, USA.

Pg. 10 ColdPlay (2016). Christmas Lights [Recorded by C. Martin]. London.

Pg. 15 Helmore, T. (1861). O Come, O Come, Emmanuel.

Pg 21 Chadwick, J. (1862). Angels, We Have Heard on High.

Pg. 28 Allen, R. (1954). Home For The Holidays [Recorded by P. Como].

Pg. 31 Allen, R. (1954). Home For The Holidays [Recorded by P. Como].

Pg. 31 Redner, L. (1868). Oh, Little Town of Bethlehem.

Pg. 33 Wesley, C. (1739). Hark, the Herald Angels Sing. London.

Pg. 33 Watts, I. (1719). Joy to the World.

Pg. 36 Traditional (n.d.). The Holly and The Ivy.

Pg. 45 Hopkins, J. H. (1857). We Three Kings.

Pg. 47 Bonhoeffer, D. (2010). *God is in the Manger*. Louisville: John Knox Press.

Pg. 50 Bott, D. (n.d.). *My little brothers: Christmas with Victor Hugo, 1862*. Retrieved from https://www.priaulxlibrary.co.uk/: https://www.priaulxlibrary.co.uk/articles/article/my-little-brothers-christmas-victor-hugo-1862

Pg. 52 Chan, J. M. (2010). Christmas in our Hearts.

Pg. 57. Buechener, F. (1991). *Telling Secrets*. San Francisco: Harper San Francisco.

Pg. 62 Watts, I. (1719). Joy to the World.

Pg. 69 Blane, R. (1944). Have Yourself A Merry Little Christmas. New York.

Pg. 77 Wells, R. (1945). Chestnuts, Roasting on an Open Fire.

Pg. 84 Oliphant, T. (1862). Deck The Halls.

Pg. 90 Redner, L. (1868). Oh, Little Town of Bethlehem.

Pg. 94 Chapman, S. C. (2009). Cinderella [Recorded by S. C. Chapman]. Nashville.

Pg. 98 Lightfoot, G. (1967). Song for a Winter's Night. New York, New York, USA.

Acknowledgements

This book is an amalgam of thoughts and conversations, ideas, and opinions. It would not have happened without the support of some exceptional humans. There are too many to mention, but it would be amiss of me to not take a moment to thank a few people who have been incredibly encouraging throughout this process:

To my dear friends at New Creation LA, especially Dan and Kerstin Myers. The community of Grace and Truth you have created is incredible. Thank you for sharing your home and your heart with me so freely over the last ten years. A random conversation with you inspired this whole book. I know there are many others out there who can look at their creative endeavours and make the same comment. This gift, to inspire and nurture creativity is a unique one, that has benefited me deeply, and for that, I will always be grateful. Also, BOB CRATCHIT!

Leah, you are simply one of the very best. Deep calls to deep friend, ours is a friendship worth fighting to protect. I hope there are brie and grape dates for years to come! Can we become rich enough to have someone do the bibliographies for us?

To Chris and Clair, my Friday night buddies, thanks for being intentional, for celebrating Christmas 2,3 and 4 at the heart of lockdown isolation. Thanks for putting up with me when my brain disappears into book writing fog in the middle of a conversation. I promise I do not do that on purpose.

Arabelle, Eleanor, Helen, Rachel, there are no words. Let us never grow tired of celebrating together. A picture where I do not look drunk or weird must be a possibility. I cannot wait for our next gathering!

Sarah, Your Greg's voice of encouragement was all over this project. I dedicated this book to his memory because he was such an influence on my creativity.

Robbie, I love our transatlantic chats. Your incredible memory for detail, and for the million times you have convinced me that what I have to say is valuable and vital. Thank You! You are quite simply, the most encouraging human that has ever existed, who is also part savage.

Andy, thanks for listening to me rant about Christmas throughout our sessions. Those moments when I appeared to forget what I was doing, in the middle of a set or, spent several minutes circling the mat; were mostly moments I was thinking about this project.

To my friends and colleagues at Urban Saints. You are above average as a group. Let the Christmas banter begin.

Finally, to my friends and family at Coventry Vineyard. What a joy it is that we get to share life. You are some of the most unique people on planet earth and I adore you all. Thanks for the privilege of walking through this world together and creating something beautiful and eternal.

About the Author

Serena McCarthy lives in Coventry, United Kingdom. She is part of the team at Coventry Vineyard and, also at Urban Saints. She lives in the Pixie Palace at the bottom of a wonderful families' garden. In her spare time, she enjoys cooking, writing, and weightlifting. That previous sentence will always make her laugh. Ultimately, she believes she is alive to tell the truth in the most beautiful way possible.

About the Illustrator

Nicky Bennett studied Fine Arts Sculpture in Loughborough University, Art PGCE at Bretton Hall. She has taught Art in England and the USA. She now home educates her two children, enjoying the world around them, living in the countryside with her beautiful little family, working hard as a home educating mum and artist. If you can't tell... She LOVES it.

Printed in Great Britain
by Amazon

69567317R00068